Passing Psychometric Tests

'Andrea Shavick's insightful book . . . is the only tome with 35 different genuine practice tests.' *The Guardian*

'A very good aid for those who might find themselves facing a psychometric questionnaire.' *Irish Examiner*

Passing Psychometric Tests

Know what to expect and get the job you want

Andrea Shavick

howtobooks

Published by How To Books Ltd,
3 Newtec Place, Magdalen Road,
Oxford OX4 1RE. United Kingdom.
Tel: (01865) 793806. Fax: (01865) 248780.
email: info@howtobooks.co.uk
http://www.howtobooks.co.uk

First edition 2002
Reprinted and revised 2003
Reprinted 2003
Reprinted 2004

British Library Cataloguing in Publication Data
A catalogue record for this book is available from the British Library

Cover design by Baseline Arts Ltd, Oxford
Produced for How To Books by Deer Park Productions, Tavistock
Typeset by PDQ Typesetting, Newcastle-under-Lyme, Staffs.
Printed and bound by Bell & Bain Ltd, Glasgow

Contents

Acknowledgements

My thanks to the following people for their help and advice: Ben Maynard and Roy Davies of SHL Group plc, Graham Shavick of Sainsbury's Supermarkets Ltd, Gus Mackintosh of One Click HR, Mark Greenberg of BACS, and Nikki Read at How To Books.

Introduction

There are three things you have to do if you want to pass a psychometric test.

No. 1 perhaps the most important thing of all, is **don't panic**. By the very act of buying this book you've already upped your chances of passing by a very long way. Familiarisation is the name of the game, and if you know what to expect, you can reduce the fear factor considerably.

No. 2 is slightly obvious (although not to everyone) and that is to **practise**. It's amazing how far you can improve your test scores with a bit of practice, especially if you haven't taken many psychometric tests before.

No. 3 is to **cheat**. Well, not literally. I'm not advocating taking binoculars into the test and stealing the other candidates' answers (although it's rather an enticing idea). But what if you could find out in advance what you'll be up against? What if you could find out exactly what type of test you'll be taking and what the pass mark is? Surely that would give you the edge over all the other applicants?

Not cheating at all really. Actually it's extremely sensible, not to mention easy, and I'm going to show you how to do it.

In this book I explain all there is to know about psychometric tests; what they are, what they measure, who uses them, why they're used, how they're changing, how to survive them, and even how to avoid them altogether!

And because the whole point of this book is to familiarise you with the different types of test and give you the chance to practise (thereby helping you improve your performance) I include **35 practice tests!**

These are not 'made up' tests that you sometimes see in books about psychometrics, nor are they puzzles or quizzes of the magazine variety. They are genuine practice tests from the biggest test publisher in the world: SHL Group plc. This is the genuine article. This is the sort of thing you'll be facing when you apply for a job with virtually any medium–large size company, irrespective of industry, whether private or public sector.

I have also given you information about the type of job (and the level) for which each test would be used, and tips on how to improve your performance with each category of test.

And if that isn't enough, I've also included a whole chapter of resources in which I have listed internet sites where you can find even more practice material, together with a list of useful books.

My aim in writing this book is to give you both knowledge and experience, not just to survive, but to pass real live psychometric tests with flying colours. Job hunting can be stressful – but not any more!

Andrea Shavick
www.shavick.com

PART ONE
What are Psychometric Tests?

CHAPTER ONE

What Are Psychometric Tests?

Psychometric tests are structured tests, taken in exam-like conditions, which aim to measure objectively a person's ability or certain aspects of their personality.

Most psychometric tests which measure ability, and virtually all accredited psychometric tests which measure aspects of personality, are devised by occupational psychologists. Their aim is twofold: to provide employers with a reliable method of selecting the best applicants, and to design tests carefully so that they are fair to all applicants.

All psychometric tests, except for personality tests, are strictly timed.

What do psychometric tests measure?

There are many different types of psychometric test. A common misconception is that psychometric tests *only* measure personality, but that is not the case.

Some measure your ability to understand the written word, or to reason with numbers. Others measure your ability to solve mechanical problems, or follow instructions accurately, or be able to understand data which is presented in a variety of ways. And then, of course, there are the personality tests, assessing everything from motivation to working preferences.

But psychometric tests cannot measure everything. For example, they can't really measure enthusiasm. Personally, I think that getting in on time every day and making an effort to do your best are to a large extent determined by how much you enjoy the actual work, how well you get on with your colleagues, and how decent your boss is. Perhaps they should invent a psychometric test for employers!

Who uses psychometric tests?

At the time of writing, well over 95% of the FTSE 100 companies use psychometric testing to select their staff, as do the police, the civil service, local authorities, the armed forces, the fire service, the National Health Service, financial institutions, retail sector companies, the motor industry, the IT industry, management consultants, airlines, the power industry – the list is endless.

In fact, virtually every large or medium-sized organisation in the UK uses psychometric testing as part of their recruitment process, irrespective of industry. Furthermore, the use of psychometric tests is widespread in Europe, Australia and the USA.

And it doesn't matter what level of job you are applying for either. Psychometric tests are used to select all types of staff, everyone from the most junior positions to director level. One thing is certain, if you are looking for a job, you are more than likely to be asked to take a psychometric test.

As to the **why** they are used – see the next chapter.

When will I have to take a psychometric test?

At any stage in the recruitment process, including first contact. These days many employers are so enthusiastic about psychometric tests, they put them on their application forms and websites.

The tests could also pop up later in the process, or even after you've been offered the job when your new boss is deciding exactly where in the organisation to place you.

How many tests will I have to take?

In theory, all psychometric tests given to job applicants should be relevant to the job. You should only have to take, for example, a spatial reasoning test if the job you are applying for requires good spatial skills.

However, many organisations use verbal, numerical and abstract reasoning tests as a matter of routine, no matter what the job description says. So be prepared to take more than one test.

Where will I have to go to take a psychometric test?

For both ability-type tests and personality questionnaires you could be examined at your potential new employer's office, at an assessment centre, at an employment agency office or even in the comfort of your own home using your computer.

Note: 'assessment centre' is HR (Human Resources/Personnel) jargon for getting candidates together – either at the employer's premises or an outside location – and subjecting them to an intensive battery of different tests and exercises. These could include role playing, in-tray exercises, group exercises and discussions, presentations and of course, psychometric tests. For more detailed information, see my book *Landing Your First Job* (details at the back of this book in Resources).

What format do the tests take?

Most psychometric tests are pencil and paper tests, but a growing number are now designed to be taken sitting at a computer console (see below). However you take the test, the format is almost always that of a multiple-choice questionnaire.

Note: Information on how tests are marked and how to record your answers is given in Chapter 3, *Taking Psychometric Tests – A Survival Guide.*

What about online testing?

Online testing is becoming increasingly common. Instead of being given a pencil and paper test, you take the test on a computer. The questions appear on the screen, and you click your answer choices with the mouse.

Within a few seconds of finishing the test, your score (for an ability test) or the analysis of your personality is emailed to the examiner.

The obvious advantage to the employer is that the candidate doesn't have to come into the office. They can take the test at the recruitment agency or even in the comfort of their own home. Instead of spending money 'entertaining' large numbers of candidates, the employer can whittle down the numbers without having to lift a finger. Another advantage for the employer is that they can test candidates anywhere in the world.

As far as you are concerned, being tested via the Internet also has its advantages. If you take a test at home, you don't need to worry about getting anywhere on time, you don't have to take a day off and you don't even need to get dressed. Plus, you should find out if the organisation is interested in taking your application any further within a few minutes, which is a million times better than waiting for them to send you a letter.

The only thing you need to do when taking a test on your home computer is make sure the person taking the test is you! If you're asked to take, say, a numerical reasoning test, resist to temptation to ask you whiz-kid brother to take it for you – you'll be found out. More on the perils of test cheating are explained in Chapter 12 on Personality Questionnaires.

Once I've got the job, will I have to take any more tests?

Quite possibly. Organisations which use tests to recruit often use them later on for internal team selection and career development of individual staff members.

Do other industries use psychometric tests?

Psychometric tests have been used for decades in two main fields other than recruitment. These are career guidance and education.

In career guidance, psychometric tests are used to help individuals gain a better understanding of their own abilities, aptitudes, interests and motivations – obviously very useful information when choosing or changing career. Here, psychometric tests are not used as a selection tool.

However, in education, it's a different ball game. Here, psychometric tests are used by many educational establishments to select the most able pupils. Every year, hundreds of thousands of children as young as 10 years old sit verbal, numerical and abstract reasoning tests in order to gain entrance to the school of their (or their parents') choice. Whole armies of after-hours teachers have for years been making a living tutoring them.

It seems that whether you're job-hunting or school-hunting, when it comes to psychometric tests, familiarisation and practice is the name of the game.

CHAPTER TWO

Why are Psychometric Tests Used?

It makes sense for an employer to find out whether an applicant is capable of doing a job *before* he or she is offered that job, for a number of reasons:

First of all, the whole process of recruiting staff is extremely expensive and time consuming. You might think it's a piece of cake, but to most employers, recruiting is a nightmare, primarily because it's so easy to pick the wrong person. Offering a job which involves figure work to a person who turns out to be unable to use a calculator would be a disaster. Employing a person in a customer service role who turns out to be incapable of problem solving and bad-tempered into the bargain, could do incalculable damage to a company's standing and reputation.

This might sound obvious, but the truth is that employers have been employing the wrong people for centuries. The difference is, in the 21st century we have tough employment laws which make it virtually impossible for companies to sack people whenever they feel like it. Employee rights, plus the very real risk of being taken to an industrial tribunal, make it even more imperative for employers to choose the right people, first time round.

The arrival of the psychometric test has been embraced by many employers because it gives them an additional tool, over and above the traditional methods of interviewing, studying CVs and taking references. Psychometric tests give employers more confidence in their ability to pick the right people.

Another reason why psychometric tests are used so extensively, especially by large organisations, is because they can be a quick, easy and relatively cheap way of eliminating large numbers of unsuitable candidates early in the recruitment process.

By 'screening out' unsuitable candidates in one fell swoop, the organisation can then concentrate on the remaining candidates in the hope of finding the 'right' people as quickly as possible.

Yet another reason why psychometric tests are so popular is because HR people like using them. From their point of view, psychometric tests have many advantages.

First of all, the use of psychometric testing can reduce their work load considerably. Why interview 100 people when, within an hour, you can whittle this number down to the 30 highest calibre candidates?

You also have to remember that HR staff are human beings, with all the same neuroses and self-doubt the rest of us have. When your job is to recruit staff (and your neck will be on the line if you make a hash of it) it's nice to have a scientific and supposedly fail-safe method at your disposal. What better way to reassure yourself that you've got it right?

If nothing else, psychometric tests give HR people (and anyone else who is involved in recruiting staff) something to talk about at an interview. This applies especially to personality tests: for example, your test might indicate you have leadership potential. Your interviewer might ask whether you agree with the test results, or ask you to describe situations in which you have used leadership skills. Not only is it useful information for them, it also makes for a more interesting and productive discussion.

Finally, not only are the tests becoming cheaper, there are now more of them to choose from. Test publishers now write psychometric tests for specific jobs, and to an individual company's particular requirements. Tailor-made tests are so common these days, you could apply to a multitude of organisations and never come up against the same test twice. You can see the attraction of using a tailor-made test – you'd feel you were getting just the right sort of person your organisation needed, not only capable of doing the job, but the right personality type to fit seamlessly into your company culture too.

Whatever the reason, the fact is that the psychometric test is a recruitment tool which is very much here to stay.

CHAPTER THREE

Taking Psychometric Tests – A Survival Guide

Hundreds of thousands of people take psychometric tests every year. This chapter is full of tips to help you feel good, boost your confidence, get you prepared and organised and generally help you survive the day of the test itself.

Before the day of the test

Find out about the test in advance

By far the most useful thing you can do to bolster your self-confidence is to get as much information about the test *in advance*.

As I said in the introduction to this book, finding out what sort of test you'll be up against and what the pass mark is, is extremely sensible and not cheating at all, even though it might feel like it!

Some companies automatically send out example questions when they invite you to take a psychometric test, but if they don't, then you need to take the initiative. Contact their HR department (or your potential new boss) and ask for more information. Ask them what sort of test you'll be taking and whether they can send you some example material.

If you get the opportunity, ask about the job and the organisation as well. Personnel managers are usually, by the very nature of their jobs, friendly and approachable, and it's extremely unlikely that they'll object to helping you. So long as you are polite and professional there is no reason why you shouldn't be successful every time.

Not only have you nothing to lose, telephoning could give you a clear advantage in more ways than one. If you know what to expect you'll be better prepared, not to mention more relaxed. And also very few of the other candidates will do it. From the employer's point of view, you will have become a candidate who is showing interest – exactly the sort of person they want.

Get directions

Make sure you've got the exact address and good directions. If you are going to drive, ring the organisation and ask them where you can park. If they suggest you use the meters or pay-and-display round the corner, don't forget to bring some change.

Get organised

Decide what you're going to wear *before* the day in question (see **Look smart**, below). I nearly missed an interview once because I spent so long trying on different outfits. For some strange reason, time speeds up considerably when you're late. Shine your shoes, sort out your briefcase, find your glasses, and if you're staying overnight at an assessment centre, pack your overnight bag...very carefully. The last thing you'll want is to discover you've forgotten your toothbrush.

Relax

Laughter is a great cure for nervous tension, so perhaps rent an amusing DVD or go to the cinema, but not the late show – you'll need a good night's sleep. Alternatively, get some exercise and follow it up with a long soak in the bath.

On the day of the test

Eat a good breakfast

Include simple sugars (fruit juice) and complex carbohydrates (toast or cereal) and possibly some protein (milk, eggs, cheese, meat). This will keep your blood sugar stable and your energy levels up.

Look smart

One of the best ways to boost your self-confidence is to look smart. If you look good and you know it, you'll feel good too. Treat the psychometric test as if you're going along to an interview, and dress accordingly. Even if you're absolutely certain that you're not going to have a face-to-face interview on the same day, it's still important to make an effort with your appearance. You'll feel better for it too.

Overestimate your journey time

If you're driving, plan the route and allow extra time for tractors, jack-knifed lorries and those awful temporary traffic lights which seem to materialise overnight. The same applies to bus and rail journeys. Trust me, if a bus or train is going to cancelled, it'll be yours.

If you are being tested alongside other candidates, you will most likely to have been given a start time for the test. If you arrive late, everyone else will have already begun and the organisation will be reluctant to disturb them by allowing you into the room. To put it bluntly – **arrive late and you probably won't be allowed to take the test at all.**

Besides, think about the impression your lateness will make on your prospective employer. They'll think, 'If he's late today, think how terrible his timekeeping will be if he gets the job.'

Smile

When you arrive, always be polite and friendly. Smile, and people will smile back at you. You'll *look* confident, even if your knees are shaking.

Stay cool

And what if your knees *are* shaking? Here are a few relaxation exercises that will help you handle the stress. With a little practice, you'll be able to use them anywhere; in the car, on the bus, in the exam room, etc.

1. **Breathing exercise**
    Breathe in slowly to really fill your lungs. Hold your breath for three seconds, then slowly breathe out through your mouth. As you breathe out, imagine all the tension and stress flowing out with the air. Repeat two or three times.

2. **Tension release exercise No. 1**
    Tense the muscle groups one by one, and then relax them. Begin with your feet: screw up your toes as tightly as possible and hold for three or four seconds. Then slowly relax. Continue upwards through your body, working your legs, your stomach, your hands, your arms, your shoulders and even your face.

3. **Tension release exercise No. 2**
    This is a good last-minute exercise to use while you're waiting to be called into the test room. Simply go to the bathroom, make sure no one can see you (you don't want an audience for this) and make yourself shake like a jelly. I mean really, physically shake

your whole body for at least 20 seconds. Pretend you're auditioning for a low-budget horror movie, then stop, take a few slow, deep breaths, and off you go. I guarantee you'll suddenly feel incredibly calm and composed and ready for anything.

Surviving the test

Listen carefully

Listen very carefully to the test administrator's instructions. Pay particular attention to what they say about the end of the test. Unlike academic exams, the administrator may not be allowed to warn candidates that time's nearly up.

Ask questions first

If there is anything about the test instructions you do not understand, or you have any other problem at all, then the time to ask is *before* it starts. Once the clock is ticking no interruptions will be allowed, although it's probably acceptable to tell the administrator that half your test paper is missing. (It wouldn't be the first time.)

If you are taking the test using a computer, make sure you know whether the answers can be changed once selected, and how you go about doing it.

Check out the paper

Instead of plunging straight into the test, have a quick look though the paper so you can see what you're up against. Is there a separate answer sheet? How many questions are there? How many different sections? Plenty of people have sat smugly in an exam room only to discover, right at the last minute, that they've missed out the last page. That really is a horrible feeling, but by checking out the paper first you won't have a problem.

Pace yourself

Pacing yourself is all about working through the paper at the right speed. Too fast and your accuracy will suffer. Too slow and you'll run out of time.

Once you've looked at the test paper, try to estimate how much time you have to answer each question, for example 50 questions in 25 minutes equals 30 seconds each.

Once you've done this you'll know that after 10 minutes you should have tackled around 20 questions, and after 20 minutes you should have tackled around 40 questions and so on. As you work through the paper, check your progress from time to time. This should ensure you never get too far behind and also reassure you that you're doing OK.

Some people even advise scribbling the desired 'finish time' for each section right there on the test paper to remind you to check the clock as you work through the test. Personally I think this takes up too much valuable time, but it could be a trick that works for you.

Note: Sometimes the tests get harder as you go along, so consider leaving more time for later questions.

One tricky situation that can occur is when you come up against a question that you simply cannot answer. If you only have around 30 seconds per question, you can see that spending 10 minutes on one of them is a bad idea. So if you get stuck, don't give yourself a hard time, simply give it up and move on. If you make a tiny mark next to the unanswered question (or ring the question number) you'll be able to see at a glance which questions still need tackling. If you have any time at the end, you can go back and try again.

Read the questions

Read each question carefully so you know exactly what information you are being asked for. This might sound obvious, but when you're under stress it's tempting to rush and not bother to check what you're being asked to do.

Many people (myself included) are so used to scanning through chunks of text at high speed, they find reading every single word with concentration incredibly difficult.

Work through the questions in order

Some people skip through test papers looking for questions they know they'll be able to answer easily. The trouble with this is that it wastes time, it's better to work through the paper in order. As I explained above, if you can't answer a question, mark it and move on to the next one.

Record your answers as instructed

Most psychometric tests are multiple choice format. This means you will be given four or five possible answer choices for each question – you have to decide which is the correct one and mark the corresponding box or circle accordingly. An example of how to do this will usually be given at the beginning of the paper.

It is vitally important that you follow these directions precisely. If you are asked to fill in the box or circle, **fill it in completely**. Don't just make a little squiggle inside it, or tick it or put a cross through it.

Most psychometric tests are marked by computers using a technique called optical marking. By indicating your answers in the correct way, the computer will be able to 'read' them. If you don't follow the instructions as requested, the computer might not be able to 'read' them and you'll lose points – even if your answers are correct.

The same goes for the *number* of answers required. If you are asked to mark one circle, mark *only* one circle. If you mark two, the computer won't know which is your intended correct answer, and you'll lose a mark, even if one of the answers is correct.

The same advice also goes for tests taken on a computer, although generally the program will not allow you to click more than one answer choice.

Concentrate

Many people find it difficult to concentrate intensely for long periods of time. It isn't easy to block out everything around you and work non-stop for up to an hour without a break.

Even if you are working in a quiet room without disturbance, your mind can start to play tricks on you. I find that I begin well, but after a few minutes my mind starts to wander. I begin to think about virtually anything else in the world other than the test. What shall I make for supper? Did I remember to programme the video? Did I lock the car? Is everyone else miles ahead of me? Why won't the guy in front stop sniffing?

The best way to combat this is to take a very short break. Sit up straight, shut your eyes and take two or three long slow breaths (see the breathing exercise above, under **Stay cool**). Or try keeping your eyes open and focusing at a point in the distance for about ten seconds.

Use tried and tested exam techniques

- Try to work out the correct answer before looking at any of the answer choices. That way, even if you can't come up with a definite answer, you'll be able to make an educated guess.

- Narrow your choices by immediately eliminating answers you can see are incorrect.

◆ If you think a question could be a 'trick' question, think again. Psychometric tests are always straightforward, there are never questions intended to deceive. It could be that you're reading too much into the question; instead try to take it at face value.

◆ Only change your answer if you are absolutely sure you have answered incorrectly. First answers are usually the correct ones.

◆ Keep working through the paper at a steady pace, keeping an eye on the clock.

Don't panic

You're almost out of time and you've got that horrible sinking feeling that says, 'Help! I'm not going to finish!' Don't panic. Instead, reassure yourself with these facts:

1. You don't have to score 100% to pass. In fact, many organisations set the 'pass' level as low as 50%. The whole point of the test is to eliminate candidates who are totally hopeless, so they can concentrate on the rest of you.

2. Many ability-type tests are not designed to be finished in the time set. Giving you more questions than you can reasonably cope with in the allotted time is a deliberate ploy. Taking a psychometric test is meant to be stressful! Afterwards, if any of the other candidates boast about finishing 15 minutes ahead of the rest of the room they're probably lying.

3. Finally, remember that if you are taking a personality test – there are no wrong answers. With a maths test there is definitely a right and a wrong answer, but with a personality test there isn't any such thing. There's more information on this later in the book.

PART TWO
The Practice Tests

Introduction

Everyone is different. If you think about it, all the people you know have different skills. Some of them are fluent communicators. Some of them have great technical ability. Some are creative. Some are innovative. Some of them can solve complicated number problems quicker than ordinary mortals eat chocolate.

But here's the catch: nobody is good at everything. Almost all of us have areas in which we are not very adept. As a writer, my ability to communicate in writing is pretty reasonable, (well, my mum thinks so anyway). But ask me to change a light bulb, or calculate my car's petrol consumption and I'm lost.

The reason I'm telling you this is because what follows is a vast selection of practice psychometric tests. Some of them you'll find easy, but others will give you more of a problem. Some of the technical tests fox me, even with the answers right in front of my nose!

So whatever you do, don't despair if you find some (or even whole sections) of the questions difficult. You certainly won't be the only one. Remember, **the whole point of this book is to familiarise yourself with the different types of test and give yourself the chance to practise, thereby helping you improve your performance.**

Note: Wherever you have difficulty with the questions, analysing them with the answers in front of you should make things clearer.

How the practice tests are arranged

The different types of psychometric test are arranged in separate chapters. In general, the easiest tests appear at the beginning of each chapter, progressing to the most difficult, or highest level tests at the end. For each test I explain:

✓ what kind of skills or abilities are being measured
✓ for what kind of job you might encounter that particular type of test.

At the end of each chapter I include a section dedicated to helping you improve your performance – and the answers.

How to get the best out of this book

To get the best out this book, treat the practice tests as if you were taking them in a real live interview. In other words, sit somewhere quiet, without distractions, and work as quickly, as accurately, and with as much concentration as you can. Record your answer choices in pencil by filling in completely the appropriate circles on the Answer Sheet (there is one for each test). This will familiarise you with the technique for recording your answers.

Time limits

Almost all of the practice tests have suggested time limits. Set the clock, and attempt as many questions as you can in the time allowed, but don't worry if you can't complete all the questions. In the real world, *psychometric tests always have more questions than most people can handle*. It's a deliberate ploy to put you under pressure, to see how you work when under stress. Besides, working under a time constraint is good experience in itself.

Of course, there's nothing to stop you giving yourself more time, or attempting the questions as many times as you like.

Concentrating

You can also work through each test in its entirety, if for no other reason than to train your brain to concentrate. Remember that these tests are **practice tests** – when you apply for a job, the psychometric tests you'll take will generally be longer, with more questions. Getting used to concentrating for longer periods of time will stand you in good stead and give you an advantage over the other candidates.

If you want to practise a particular type of test, the following list will help you locate the one you want quickly:

Numerical Reasoning Tests

Abstract Reasoning Tests

Spatial Reasoning Tests

Mechanical Comprehension Tests

Fault Diagnosis Tests

Accuracy Tests

Combination Tests

Personality Test Questionnaires

Remember – familiarisation and practice is the name of the game! Good luck.

Verbal Reasoning

Verbal reasoning tests are multiple choice tests which measure your ability to reason with words. They are widely used in recruitment to select staff, simply because the ability to understand the written word is an essential skill for most jobs.

The simplest verbal reasoning tests assess your basic language skills: spelling, vocabulary and understanding of grammar. You are usually presented with four or five different words, or groups of words, and asked to pick the ones which:

✓ are spelt correctly

✓ are spelt incorrectly

✓ do not belong in the group

✓ mean the same

✓ mean the opposite

✓ best complete a sentence

✓ best fill the gaps in a sentence.

Analogies are also popular. Artist is to painting, as author is to_____.

A. keyboard

B. publisher

C. book

D. bicycle

What's being tested is your ability to recognise relationships between words. If an artist *creates* a painting, what might an author create? The correct answer is C.

Higher-level tests not only measure language skills, they examine your ability to make sense of, and logically evaluate, the written word. These tests are often called **critical reasoning** tests, but in essence they are comprehension exercises. In each case you are required to read a short text, or passage and then answer questions about it.

However, unlike the comprehension exercises that you did in school, where the answers were obvious so long as you read the text carefully enough, critical reasoning tests generally require a little more brain power.

You are often asked to decide whether a statement is true or false, or impossible to verify, *given the information contained in the passage*. This last phrase is very important. Not only are you being forced to think very carefully about what you have read, you must endeavour not to make any assumptions about it. You must answer the question using only the given information – something which is surprisingly difficult to do if you have any knowledge of (or an opinion on) the subject matter in question. Remember, it is only your ability to understand and make logical deductions from the passage that is being tested, not your knowledge of the subject matter.

The vocabulary and subject of the passage are often similar to those encountered in the actual job for which you are applying. For example, if you are applying for a technical job in IT, then any verbal reasoning test you encounter is quite likely to include the language, vocabulary and jargon prevalent in that industry.

All verbal reasoning psychometric tests are strictly timed, and *each question will have one, and only one correct answer.*

In this chapter

In this chapter there are seven different verbal reasoning practice tests for you to try. Before each one I've indicated for what sort of job (and at what level) you might be expected to take that particular type of test.

At the end of the chapter there is section entitled **How to improve your performance** which is intended to help you do just that across the whole range of verbal reasoning tests. Included in this section are some hints on tackling the questions themselves. If you have a problem with any of the questions then hopefully the advice contained in this section will get you back on track. Remember, however, that all of us have strengths and weaknesses, and everyone will have some difficulty with some of the tests in this book.

Test 1 Verbal Usage

The first of the verbal reasoning tests measures your vocabulary, spelling and grammatical skills, and also your understanding of written information. This type of test is often used to select clerical and administrative staff at all levels.

Instructions: In each question, choose the pair of words which best complete each sentence. Indicate your answer each time by filling in completely the appropriate circle on the answer sheet.

Time guideline: There are 8 questions – see how many you can do in 3 minutes.

---

1 Now the company had the _____ to beat its main _____

A	B	C	D	E
opportunity	opportunity	opportounity	opportounity	NONE OF
competittor	competitor	competittor	competitor	THESE

---

2 This _____ has given us many _____ for improving our products.

A	B	C	D	E
client	cliant	client	cliant	NONE OF
suggestions	suggestions	sugestions	sugestions	THESE

---

3 Results like these _____ on careful _____

A	B	C	D	E
dipend	dipend	dipends	dipends	NONE OF
implementation	implimentation	implementation	implimentation	THESE

---

4 _____ the attack that had been made on him, his speech was _____

A	B	C	D	E
Considering	Considering	considering	considering	NONE OF
moderate	modarate	moderate	modarate	THESE

| 5 | The [   ] letter included many elaborate [   ] |

	A	B	C	D	E
	original	original	originel	originel	NONE OF
	sentences	sentence	sentences	sentance	THESE

| 6 | I agree [   ] your contention that the [   ] should be favourably considered. |

	A	B	C	D	E
	with	with	to	to	NONE OF
	aplication	application	aplication	application	THESE

| 7 | Costs are to be [   ] by [   ] |

	A	B	C	D	E
	repayed	repayed	repaid	repaid	NONE OF
	instalments	instalments	instalments	instalments	THESE

| 8 | The [   ] is [   ] if you do not pay the premium on time. |

	A	B	C	D	E
	pollicy	pollicy	polisy	polisy	NONE OF
	forfieted	forfeated	forfieted	forfeated	THESE

Test 1 Answer Sheet

	A	B	C	D	E
1	Ⓐ	Ⓑ	Ⓒ	Ⓓ	Ⓔ
2	Ⓐ	Ⓑ	Ⓒ	Ⓓ	Ⓔ
3	Ⓐ	Ⓑ	Ⓒ	Ⓓ	Ⓔ
4	Ⓐ	Ⓑ	Ⓒ	Ⓓ	Ⓔ
5	Ⓐ	Ⓑ	Ⓒ	Ⓓ	Ⓔ
6	Ⓐ	Ⓑ	Ⓒ	Ⓓ	Ⓔ
7	Ⓐ	Ⓑ	Ⓒ	Ⓓ	Ⓔ
8	Ⓐ	Ⓑ	Ⓒ	Ⓓ	Ⓔ

Test 2 Verbal Comprehension

This test measures your vocabulary and basic word skills using language which reflects the requirements of technical occupations.

This type of test is often used to select staff in technically or practically orientated jobs, for example, craft apprentices, technical apprentices, skilled operatives and technical supervisors.

Instructions: In each question, choose the correct answer from the five possible answers, indicating this each time by filling in completely the appropriate circle on the answer sheet.

Time guideline: There are 8 questions – see how many you can do in 3 minutes.

Choose the word which **best** completes the following sentence.

| 1 | All employees should [   ] from such a training scheme. |

A	B	C	D	E
result	credit	succeed	enrol	benefit

| 2 | Hard is to soft as hot is to [   ] |

A	B	C	D	E
cool	warm	cold	icy	tepid

| 3 | Which of the following words is closest in meaning to toxic? |

A	B	C	D	E
putrid	poisonous	bitter	contagious	inedible

Choose the word which **best** completes the following sentences.

| 4 | All exposed pipes will have to be [_____] to protect them from freezing. |

A	B	C	D	E
insulated	regulated	connected	incorporated	hot

| 5 | Which of the following words is closest in meaning to vertical? |

A	B	C	D	E
horizontal	parallel	straight	perpendicular	flat

| 6 | Stay is to leave as advance is to [_____] |

A	B	C	D	E
arrive	exit	retreat	come	hold

Choose the word which **best** completes the following sentences

| 7 | A straight-edge should be used to ensure that the ends of the shelves are correctly [_____] |

A	B	C	D	E
tightened	aligned	concentric	separated	flat

| 8 | Adept means the same as: |

A	B	C	D	E
energetic	inefficient	enthusiastic	awkward	skilful

Test 2 Answer Sheet

	A	B	C	D	E
1	Ⓐ	Ⓑ	Ⓒ	Ⓓ	Ⓔ
2	Ⓐ	Ⓑ	Ⓒ	Ⓓ	Ⓔ
3	Ⓐ	Ⓑ	Ⓒ	Ⓓ	Ⓔ
4	Ⓐ	Ⓑ	Ⓒ	Ⓓ	Ⓔ
5	Ⓐ	Ⓑ	Ⓒ	Ⓓ	Ⓔ
6	Ⓐ	Ⓑ	Ⓒ	Ⓓ	Ⓔ
7	Ⓐ	Ⓑ	Ⓒ	Ⓓ	Ⓔ
8	Ⓐ	Ⓑ	Ⓒ	Ⓓ	Ⓔ

Test 3 Verbal Comprehension

This test measures your ability to interpret and understand written information. It requires a higher level of verbal skills than the previous tests.

This type of test is often used in the selection of individuals for clerical and administrative staff at all levels, for example, clerical staff, staff administrators, staff supervisors, secretaries and WP operators.

Instructions: In this test you are required to evaluate each statement in the light of the passage preceding it. Read through the passage and evaluate the statements according to the rules below.

Mark circle A if the statement is true given the information in the passage.

Mark circle B if the statement is false given the information in the passage.

Mark circle C if you cannot say whether the statement is true or false without further information.

Indicate your answer each time by filling in completely the appropriate circle on the answer sheet.

Time guideline: There is no official time guideline for this practice test, however, try to work through the questions as quickly as you can.

The cafeteria is open at 7am.
Lunch is served between 11.30am and 2.30pm. If you require a meal after 2.30pm you must tell the chef before 2pm. Guests may be brought into the cafeteria if a special pass has been obtained from the Catering Manager.

---

1 The cafeteria is open at breakfast time.

2 You can have lunch at 1.30pm if you wish.

3 If you want a meal after 2.30pm, you must inform the Catering Manager.

4 The cafeteria is strictly for members of staff only.

All clerical staff should use form FPM2 to annually renew their security pass unless they wish to change any personal details. In this case, they should use either form FPM1 or FMP3. Form FPM1 should be used when staff members have been promoted, whereas form FPM3 should be used if other personal details have been changed, eg, address, department etc. Lost security passes must be replaced using form GMP2. The supervisor will supply this form when he/she is informed of the loss of the pass.

5 Mrs Jeffrey has lost her security pass. She should fill in form GPM2 to obtain a new one.

6 Form FPM3 should not be used to renew a security pass following a promotion.

7 Mr McCarthy has changed his address within the last twelve months. He should fill in form FPM2.

8 Staff must pay to have lost security passes replaced.

Test 3 Answer Sheet

	A	B	C
1	Ⓐ	Ⓑ	Ⓒ
2	Ⓐ	Ⓑ	Ⓒ
3	Ⓐ	Ⓑ	Ⓒ
4	Ⓐ	Ⓑ	Ⓒ
5	Ⓐ	Ⓑ	Ⓒ
6	Ⓐ	Ⓑ	Ⓒ
7	Ⓐ	Ⓑ	Ⓒ
8	Ⓐ	Ⓑ	Ⓒ

Test 4 Verbal Reasoning

This test measures your ability to evaluate the logic of written information. It is designed for staff who need to understand and interpret written material with a technical context.

This type of test is designed for the selection, development and promotion of staff working in Information Technology and is suitable for applicants with A levels to graduate qualification or equivalent.

Instructions: In this test you are given two passages, each of which is followed by several statements. You are required to evaluate the statements in the light of the information or opinions contained in the passage and select your answer according to the rules below:

Mark circle A if the statement is patently **true**, or follows logically *given the information in the passage.*

Mark circle B if the statement is patently **untrue**, or if the opposite follows logically, *given the information in the passage.*

Mark circle C if you **cannot say** whether the statement is true or follows logically *without further information.*

Indicate your answer each time by filling in completely the appropriate circle on the answer sheet.

Time guideline: See how many questions you can complete in 5 minutes.

Among the useful features available on this computer system is the **Notebk** feature. The **Notebk** feature organises lists of information in a record format. Its most obvious use is for lists of names, phone numbers and addresses but many other applications can be defined. One of the biggest advantages of using **Notebk** is that the files are stored in a format that can be used directly by other features. This means that files do not have to be converted or altered in any way.

---

1   The **Notebk** feature can only be used to organise lists of names, phone numbers and addresses.

2   If users wish to use **Notebk** files with other features, they do not need to alter the files.

3   The **Notebk** feature enables the user to instantly update lists of names and addresses.

Software engineering is an approach to the improvement of system productivity. In most circumstances, it has a modest impact on the productivity of the system during the initial development stage. However, systems developed using software engineering techniques have substantially lower maintenance costs and higher reliability.

4   Lower maintenance costs can be expected if the system used was developed using software engineering techniques.

5   Systems developed with these techniques are more likely to break down.

6   Software engineering is a widely used methodology when developing new systems.

Test 4 Answer Sheet

	A	B	C
1	Ⓐ	Ⓑ	Ⓒ
2	Ⓐ	Ⓑ	Ⓒ
3	Ⓐ	Ⓑ	Ⓒ
4	Ⓐ	Ⓑ	Ⓒ
5	Ⓐ	Ⓑ	Ⓒ
6	Ⓐ	Ⓑ	Ⓒ

Test 5 Verbal Evaluation

This test measures your ability to understand and evaluate the logic of various kinds of argument.

This type of test is often used to assess reasoning skills at administrative, supervisory and junior management levels. It could be used to select applicants for a wide range of jobs, for example, office supervisor, senior personal assistant, sales and customer service staff, junior managers and management trainees.

Instructions: In this test you are required to evaluate each statement in the light of the passage and select your answer according to the rules below:

Mark circle A if the statement follows logically from *the information or opinions contained in the passage.*

Mark circle B if the statement is obviously false from *the information or opinions contained in the passage.*

Mark circle C if you cannot say whether the statement is true or false *without further information*.

Indicate your answer each time by filling in completely the appropriate circle on the answer sheet.

Time guideline: See how many questions you can complete in 5 minutes.

> Many organisations find it beneficial to employ students during the summer. Permanent staff often wish to take their own holidays over this period. Furthermore, it is not uncommon for companies to experience peak workloads in the summer and so require extra staff. Summer employment also attracts students who may return as well qualified recruits to an organisation when they have completed their education. Ensuring that the students learn as much as possible about the organisation encourages their interest in working on a permanent basis. Organisations pay students on a fixed rate without the usual entitlement to paid holidays or sick leave.

1   It is possible that permanent staff who are on holiday can have their work carried out by students.

2   Students in summer employment are given the same paid holiday benefit as permanent staff.

3   Students are subject to the organisation's standard disciplinary and grievance procedures.

4   Some companies have more work to do in summer when students are available for vacation work.

Most banks and building societies adopt a 'no smoking' policy in customer areas in their branches. Plaques and stickers are displayed in these areas to draw attention to this policy. The notices are worded in a 'customer friendly' manner, though a few customers may feel their personal freedom of choice is being infringed. If a customer does ignore a notice, staff are tolerant and avoid making a great issue of the situation. In fact, the majority of customers now expect a 'no smoking' policy in premises of this kind. After all, such a policy improves the pleasantness of the customer facilities and also lessens fire risk.

5   'No smoking' policies have mainly been introduced in response to customer demand.

6   All banks and building societies now have a 'no smoking' policy.

7   There is no conflict of interest between a 'no smoking' policy and personal freedom of choice for all.

8   A no-smoking policy is in line with most customers' expectations in banks and building societies.

Test 5 Answer Sheet

	A	B	C
1	Ⓐ	Ⓑ	Ⓒ
2	Ⓐ	Ⓑ	Ⓒ
3	Ⓐ	Ⓑ	Ⓒ
4	Ⓐ	Ⓑ	Ⓒ
5	Ⓐ	Ⓑ	Ⓒ
6	Ⓐ	Ⓑ	Ⓒ
7	Ⓐ	Ⓑ	Ⓒ
8	Ⓐ	Ⓑ	Ⓒ

Test 6 Technical Understanding

This test measures your ability to understand a written passage containing the type of material likely to be found in a typical technical setting, such as machine manuals and operating instructions.

This type of test is often used in the selection and development of individuals in technically or practically orientated jobs, such as craft apprenticeships, technical apprentices, skilled operative and technical supervisors.

Instructions: You are required to read the passage carefully, then, using the information provided, answer the questions which follow. Indicate your answer each time by filling in completely the appropriate circle on the answer sheet.

Time guideline: See how many questions you can complete in 2 minutes.

Company van use/allocation codes

Three codes exist for company vans:

001 – possess company van with full expenses paid
002 – possess company van with partial expenses paid
003 – has the facility to borrow a company van
004 – does not have the facility to borrow a company van

All senior members have 001 codes; 002 codes are automatically given to non-senior members after 2 years of relevant service and 003 codes exist for members who have not been with the company for two years but whose jobs include a high driving element. People with 004 codes tend to be those without a driving licence or individuals who rarely have the need for a van.

---

1   Which code would a senior member with two years service have?

A) 001.

B) 002.

C) 003.

D) 004.

2   Members who only have one year of service but spend a large part of their time driving, would have which code?

A) 001.

B) 002.

C) 003.

D) 004.

3   Which facility is unique to code 002?

A) The company van.

B) Partial expenses.

C) Full expenses.

D) A borrowing facility.

4   An individual who has worked for the company for three years but who does not drive would be given what code?

A) 001.

B) 002.

C) 003.

D) 004.

Test 6 Answer Sheet

	A	B	C	D
1	Ⓐ	Ⓑ	Ⓒ	Ⓓ
2	Ⓐ	Ⓑ	Ⓒ	Ⓓ
3	Ⓐ	Ⓑ	Ⓒ	Ⓓ
4	Ⓐ	Ⓑ	Ⓒ	Ⓓ

Test 7 Verbal Test

This test measures your ability to evaluate the logic of written information. This type of test is used for the selection of graduates over a wide range of industries. It can also be used in the selection and development of work-experienced managers, professional staff, middle managers and senior managers.

Instructions: In this test you are given two passages, each of which is followed by several statements. You are required to evaluate the statements in the light of the information or opinions contained in the passage and select your answer according to the rules given below:

Mark circle A if the statement is patently **true**, or follows logically *given the information or opinions contained in the passage.*

Mark circle B if the statement is patently **untrue**, or if the opposite follows logically, *given the information or opinions contained in the passage.*

Mark circle C if you **cannot say** whether the statement is true or untrue or follows logically *without further information.*

Indicate your answer each time by filling in completely the appropriate circle on the answer sheet.

Time guideline: There is no official time guideline for this practice test, however, try to work through the questions as quickly as you can.

> The big economic difference between nuclear and fossil-fuelled power stations is that nuclear reactors are more expensive to build and decommission, but cheaper to run. So disputes over the relative efficiency of the two systems revolve not just around the prices of coal and uranium today and tomorrow, but also around the way in which future income should be compared with current income.

1   The main difference between nuclear and fossil-fuelled power stations is an economic one.

2   The price of coal is not relevant to discussions about the relative efficiency of nuclear reactors.

3   If nuclear reactors were cheaper to build and decommission than fossil-fuelled power stations, they would definitely have the economic advantage.

At any given moment we are being bombarded by physical and psychological stimuli competing for our attention. Although our eyes are capable of handling more than 5 million bits of data per second, our brains are capable of interpreting only about 500 bits per second. With similar disparities between each of the other senses and the brain, it is easy to see that we must select the visual, auditory, or tactile stimuli that we wish to compute at any specific time.

4 Physical stimuli usually win in the competition for our attention.

5 The capacity of the human brain is sufficient to interpret nearly all the stimuli the senses can register under optimum conditions.

6 Eyes are able to cope with the greater input of information than ears.

Test 7 Answer Sheet

	A	B	C
1	Ⓐ	Ⓑ	Ⓒ
2	Ⓐ	Ⓑ	Ⓒ
3	Ⓐ	Ⓑ	Ⓒ
4	Ⓐ	Ⓑ	Ⓒ
5	Ⓐ	Ⓑ	Ⓒ
6	Ⓐ	Ⓑ	Ⓒ

Answers to verbal reasoning questions

Test 1 Verbal Usage

	A	B	C	D	E
1	Ⓐ	●	Ⓒ	Ⓓ	Ⓔ
2	●	Ⓑ	Ⓒ	Ⓓ	Ⓔ
3	Ⓐ	Ⓑ	Ⓒ	Ⓓ	●
4	●	Ⓑ	Ⓒ	Ⓓ	Ⓔ
5	●	Ⓑ	Ⓒ	Ⓓ	Ⓔ
6	Ⓐ	●	Ⓒ	Ⓓ	Ⓔ
7	Ⓐ	Ⓑ	Ⓒ	●	Ⓔ
8	Ⓐ	Ⓑ	Ⓒ	Ⓓ	●

Test 2 Verbal Comprehension

	A	B	C	D	E
1	Ⓐ	Ⓑ	Ⓒ	Ⓓ	●
2	Ⓐ	Ⓑ	●	Ⓓ	Ⓔ
3	Ⓐ	●	Ⓒ	Ⓓ	Ⓔ
4	●	Ⓑ	Ⓒ	Ⓓ	Ⓔ
5	Ⓐ	Ⓑ	Ⓒ	●	Ⓔ
6	Ⓐ	Ⓑ	●	Ⓓ	Ⓔ
7	Ⓐ	●	Ⓒ	Ⓓ	Ⓔ
8	Ⓐ	Ⓑ	Ⓒ	Ⓓ	●

Test 3 Verbal Comprehension

	A	B	C
1	●	Ⓑ	Ⓒ
2	●	Ⓑ	Ⓒ
3	Ⓐ	●	Ⓒ
4	Ⓐ	●	Ⓒ
5	●	Ⓑ	Ⓒ
6	●	Ⓑ	Ⓒ
7	Ⓐ	●	Ⓒ
8	Ⓐ	Ⓑ	●

Test 4 Verbal Reasoning

	A	B	C
1	Ⓐ	●	Ⓒ
2	●	Ⓑ	Ⓒ
3	Ⓐ	Ⓑ	●
4	●	Ⓑ	Ⓒ
5	Ⓐ	●	Ⓒ
6	Ⓐ	Ⓑ	●

Test 5 Verbal Evaluation

	A	B	C
1	●	Ⓑ	Ⓒ
2	Ⓐ	●	Ⓒ
3	Ⓐ	Ⓑ	●
4	●	Ⓑ	Ⓒ
5	Ⓐ	Ⓑ	●
6	Ⓐ	●	Ⓒ
7	Ⓐ	●	Ⓒ
8	●	Ⓑ	Ⓒ

Test 6 Technical Understanding

	A	B	C	D
1	●	Ⓑ	Ⓒ	Ⓓ
2	Ⓐ	Ⓑ	●	Ⓓ
3	Ⓐ	●	Ⓒ	Ⓓ
4	Ⓐ	Ⓑ	Ⓒ	●

Test 7 Verbal Test

	A	B	C
1	Ⓐ	Ⓑ	●
2	Ⓐ	●	Ⓒ
3	●	Ⓑ	Ⓒ
4	Ⓐ	Ⓑ	●
5	Ⓐ	●	Ⓒ
6	Ⓐ	Ⓑ	●

How to improve your performance

- In critical reasoning tests, always read the passage thoroughly. Don't skip through sections, or scan the text at high speed. Reading with understanding requires concentrated effort – not an easy thing to do however good your reading skills. Re-read anything of which you are unsure.

- Also read the questions very carefully to ensure you understand exactly what you are being asked.

- Look at the answer choices and quickly eliminate any you know to be incorrect. Concentrate your energies on deciding between the most likely possibilities.

- Think carefully before selecting an answer which includes words like *always*, *never*, *true*, *false*, *none* and *all*. These words leave no room for manoeuvre or any exception whatsoever.

- Answer the questions using only the given information. Don't let prior knowledge or your opinion on the subject matter influence you. Only your ability to understand and make logical deductions from the passage is being tested.

- Verbal reasoning tests demand a high level of concentration, so treat yourself to a break every now and then. Sit up straight, shut your eyes and take a few deep breaths, just for 20 seconds or so. This will calm you down, relax your back and give your eyes and brain a well deserved rest.

To improve general performance in verbal reasoning tests:

- Read books and newspapers.
- Do verbal problem-solving exercises like crosswords.
- Play word games like Scrabble.
- If applying for a managerial position, read reports and business journals.
- If applying for a technical job, read technical manuals and instruction books.

CHAPTER FIVE

Numerical Reasoning

Numerical reasoning tests are written, multiple-choice psychometric tests which are used as part of the selection procedure for jobs with any element of figure work. This includes a wide range of jobs, such as those dealing with money, processing invoices, buying, administration, engineering, statistics, analytical science, and any sort of numerical calculations.

Numerical reasoning questions can be presented in a variety of different ways, including:

♦ basic maths

♦ sequences

♦ number problems

♦ numerical estimation problems

♦ data interpretation using tables, graphs and diagrams

and varying levels of difficulty. Most do not allow you the use of a calculator. All numerical reasoning tests are strictly timed, and *each question will have one, and only one correct answer*.

In this chapter

In this chapter there are eight different numerical psychometric tests for you to try. Before each one I've indicated for what sort of job (and at what level) you might be expected to take that particular type of test.

At the end of the chapter there is a section entitled **How to improve your performance** which is intended to help you do just that across the whole range of numerical tests. Included in this section are some hints on tackling the questions themselves. If you have a problem with any of the questions then hopefully the advice contained in this section will get you back on track. Remember, however, that all of us have strengths and weaknesses, and everyone will have some difficulty with some of the tests in this book.

Note: Do not use a calculator unless specifically instructed to.

Test 8 Numerical Computation

The first of the numerical reasoning tests is called a **numerical computation** test, a rather fancy name for basic maths. The emphasis is on understanding numerical relationships and operations, as well as on quick and accurate calculation.

This type of test is often used in the selection and development of individuals in technically or practically orientated jobs such as craft apprentices, technical apprentices, skilled operatives and technical supervisors.

Instructions: In each question find the number which should replace the question mark. Indicate your answer by filling in completely the appropriate circle on the answer sheet. *Do not use a calculator.*

Time guideline: There are 10 questions – see how many you can do in 3 minutes. Remember to work accurately as well as quickly.

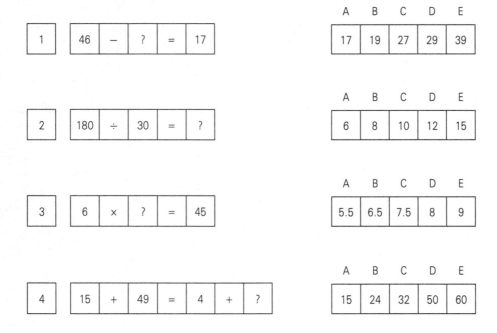

| 1 | 46 | – | ? | = | 17 |

	A	B	C	D	E
	17	19	27	29	39

| 2 | 180 | ÷ | 30 | = | ? |

	A	B	C	D	E
	6	8	10	12	15

| 3 | 6 | × | ? | = | 45 |

	A	B	C	D	E
	5.5	6.5	7.5	8	9

| 4 | 15 | + | 49 | = | 4 | + | ? |

	A	B	C	D	E
	15	24	32	50	60

5	$^3/_5$	×	?	=	$^1/_5$

	A	B	C	D	E
	$^1/_6$	$^1/_4$	$^1/_3$	$^1/_2$	$^2/_3$

6	35.6	+	2.43	=	?

	A	B	C	D	E
	37.3	38.03	38.9	39.13	39.63

7	60% of 20 =	?

	A	B	C	D	E
	12	13	14	15	16

8	0.1	×	0.1	=	?

	A	B	C	D	E
	0.0011	0.01	0.1	0.11	1.0

9	0.8	÷	0.2	=	?

	A	B	C	D	E
	0.16	0.25	0.4	4.0	16.0

10	17	×	16	=	?	×	8

	A	B	C	D	E
	18	19	25	34	40

Test 8 Answer Sheet

	A	B	C	D	E
1	Ⓐ	Ⓑ	Ⓒ	Ⓓ	Ⓔ
2	Ⓐ	Ⓑ	Ⓒ	Ⓓ	Ⓔ
3	Ⓐ	Ⓑ	Ⓒ	Ⓓ	Ⓔ
4	Ⓐ	Ⓑ	Ⓒ	Ⓓ	Ⓔ
5	Ⓐ	Ⓑ	Ⓒ	Ⓓ	Ⓔ
6	Ⓐ	Ⓑ	Ⓒ	Ⓓ	Ⓔ
7	Ⓐ	Ⓑ	Ⓒ	Ⓓ	Ⓔ
8	Ⓐ	Ⓑ	Ⓒ	Ⓓ	Ⓔ
9	Ⓐ	Ⓑ	Ⓒ	Ⓓ	Ⓔ
10	Ⓐ	Ⓑ	Ⓒ	Ⓓ	Ⓔ

Test 9 Numerical Computation

Now try another numerical computation test. This measures basic number skills with the emphasis on straightforward calculation.

This type of test is often used in the selection of individuals for clerical and administrative staff at all levels, for example, clerical staff, staff administrators, staff supervisors, secretaries and WP operators.

Instructions: As in the previous test, find the number which should replace the question mark. Indicate your answer by filling in completely the appropriate circle on the answer sheet. *Do not use a calculator.*

Time guideline: There are 9 questions – see how many you can do in 3 minutes. Remember to work accurately as well as quickly.

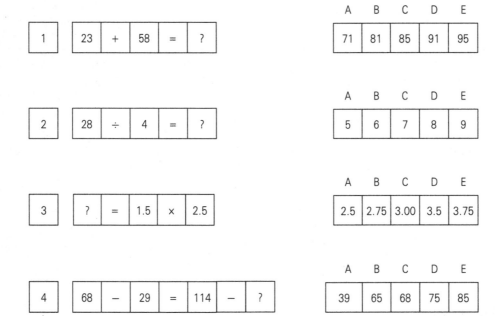

1	23	+	58	=	?

A	B	C	D	E
71	81	85	91	95

2	28	÷	4	=	?

A	B	C	D	E
5	6	7	8	9

3	?	=	1.5	×	2.5

A	B	C	D	E
2.5	2.75	3.00	3.5	3.75

4	68	–	29	=	114	–	?

A	B	C	D	E
39	65	68	75	85

| 5 | $\frac{1}{3}$ | − | $\frac{1}{5}$ | = | ? |

	A	B	C	D	E
	$\frac{1}{15}$	$\frac{1}{8}$	$\frac{2}{15}$	$\frac{1}{2}$	$\frac{3}{5}$

| 6 | 17 | × | ? | = | 204 |

	A	B	C	D	E
	9	10	11	12	13

| 7 | 132 | ÷ | ? | = | 12 |

	A	B	C	D	E
	9	9.5	10	10.5	11

| 8 | 16 | + | 25 | = | ? | + | 13 |

	A	B	C	D	E
	28	31	38	41	48

| 9 | 21 | ÷ | 3 | = | 91 | ÷ | ? |

	A	B	C	D	E
	7	9	11	12	13

Test 9 Answer Sheet

	A	B	C	D	E
1	Ⓐ	Ⓑ	Ⓒ	Ⓓ	Ⓔ
2	Ⓐ	Ⓑ	Ⓒ	Ⓓ	Ⓔ
3	Ⓐ	Ⓑ	Ⓒ	Ⓓ	Ⓔ
4	Ⓐ	Ⓑ	Ⓒ	Ⓓ	Ⓔ
5	Ⓐ	Ⓑ	Ⓒ	Ⓓ	Ⓔ
6	Ⓐ	Ⓑ	Ⓒ	Ⓓ	Ⓔ
7	Ⓐ	Ⓑ	Ⓒ	Ⓓ	Ⓔ
8	Ⓐ	Ⓑ	Ⓒ	Ⓓ	Ⓔ
9	Ⓐ	Ⓑ	Ⓒ	Ⓓ	Ⓔ

Test 10 Numerical Reasoning

In this test you are given numerical problems to solve. Your ability to reason with numbers is being measured. The test is designed for the selection of clerical and administrative staff of all types. For some tests of this nature you may be allowed to use a calculator, for others you may not.

Instructions: For each question you must choose the correct answer from five possible answers. Indicate your answer by filling in completely the appropriate circle on the answer sheet. *You may use a calculator.*

Time guideline: There are 8 questions – see how many you can do in 3 minutes *using a calculator, or 5 minutes without a calculator.*

Remember to work accurately as well as quickly.

1	If a box of pens costs £7.23, how much would 4 boxes cost?				
	A £26.46	B £26.92	C £28.46	D £28.82	E £28.92

2	What change is due from £5 when purchasing a folder priced at £2.97?				
	A £1.03	B £2.03	C £2.13	D £3.03	E £3.13

3	If 4 pads of paper weigh 0.6kg, what would 7 pads weigh?				
	A 0.15kg	B 1.05kg	C 1.10kg	D 1.15kg	E 1.5g

4	If I work from 7.45am to 3.30pm Monday to Friday, how many hours do I work in a week?				
	A 37hrs 30mins	B 37hrs 45mins	C 38hrs 15mins	D 38hrs 30mins	E 39hrs 45mins

5	A part-time office clerk earning £85 per week received a salary increase of 7%. What was the clerk's new salary?				
	A £90.95	B £91.95	C £92.00	D £92.95	E £93

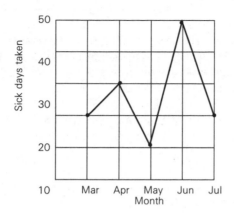

6 | From the graph, how many sick days were taken in total during May and June?

A	B	C	D	E
30	40	50	60	70

7 | From the graph, what is the average number of sick days taken between March and July inclusive?

A	B	C	D	E
20	25	26	30	36

8 | What percentage of £125 is £25?

A	B	C	D	E
12½%	15%	17½%	20%	22½%

Test 10 Answer Sheet

	A	B	C	D	E
1	Ⓐ	Ⓑ	Ⓒ	Ⓓ	Ⓔ
2	Ⓐ	Ⓑ	Ⓒ	Ⓓ	Ⓔ
3	Ⓐ	Ⓑ	Ⓒ	Ⓓ	Ⓔ
4	Ⓐ	Ⓑ	Ⓒ	Ⓓ	Ⓔ
5	Ⓐ	Ⓑ	Ⓒ	Ⓓ	Ⓔ
6	Ⓐ	Ⓑ	Ⓒ	Ⓓ	Ⓔ
7	Ⓐ	Ⓑ	Ⓒ	Ⓓ	Ⓔ
8	Ⓐ	Ⓑ	Ⓒ	Ⓓ	Ⓔ

Test 11 Numerical Reasoning

In this test you are given numerical problems to solve. All the questions have a technical bias, and can be used in the selection and development of individuals in technically or practically orientated jobs such as craft apprentices, skilled operatives and technical supervisors, or any job in a technical field which involves an element of figure work or calculation.

Instructions: For each question you must choose the correct answer from five possible answers. Indicate your answer by filling in completely the appropriate circle on the answer sheet. *You may use a calculator.*

Time guideline: There are 6 questions – see how many you can do in 3 minutes using a calculator. Remember to work accurately as well as quickly.

1. | If 1,000 ball bearings cost £42.50, how much would 2,300 cost? | | | | |
   |---|---|---|---|---|
   | A | B | C | D | E |
   | £85 | £97.75 | £105.50 | £110.25 | £125.50 |

2. | How many rivets are needed to attach a 10cm brass plate if one rivet is inserted evey 4mm (10mm = 1cm)? | | | | |
   |---|---|---|---|---|
   | A | B | C | D | E |
   | 5 | 15 | 25 | 250 | 500 |

3. | When totally full, a barrel contains 75 litres of oil. How many litres of oil remain if 40% has been used? | | | | |
   |---|---|---|---|---|
   | A | B | C | D | E |
   | 1.25 litres | 30 litres | 45 litres | 60 litres | 75 litres |

4. | A press stamps out 5 components every minute. How many components would be cut out in 8 hours if the same rate was maintained? | | | | |
   |---|---|---|---|---|
   | A | B | C | D | E |
   | 96 | 300 | 600 | 2,400 | 5,760 |

5 | What is the area of the steel plate shown below?

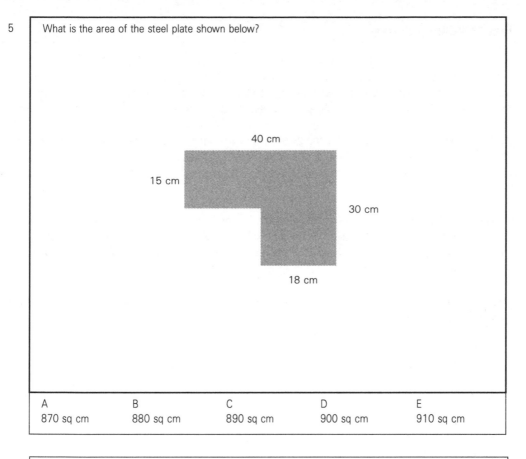

40 cm

15 cm

30 cm

18 cm

A	B	C	D	E
870 sq cm	880 sq cm	890 sq cm	900 sq cm	910 sq cm

6 | A piece of timber has been cut into two lengths in the ratio of 7:2. If the original piece of timber was 828 cm long, how long is the larger of the cut lengths?

A	B	C	D	E
118 cm	184 cm	591 cm	600 cm	644 cm

Test 11 Answer Sheet

	A	B	C	D	E
1	Ⓐ	Ⓑ	Ⓒ	Ⓓ	Ⓔ
2	Ⓐ	Ⓑ	Ⓒ	Ⓓ	Ⓔ
3	Ⓐ	Ⓑ	Ⓒ	Ⓓ	Ⓔ
4	Ⓐ	Ⓑ	Ⓒ	Ⓓ	Ⓔ
5	Ⓐ	Ⓑ	Ⓒ	Ⓓ	Ⓔ
6	Ⓐ	Ⓑ	Ⓒ	Ⓓ	Ⓔ

Test 12 Number Series

The following problems are presented as sequences. They measure your ability to reason with numbers. In particular, this test assesses your ability to develop strategies and to recognise the relationships between numbers. Some of the questions are straightforward, others are a little more complicated.

This type of test is designed for the selection, development and promotion of staff working in Information Technology, for example, software engineers, systems analysts, programmers and database administrators, and for any IT job where the recognition of numerical relationships or sequences is important.

Instructions: Each problem in the test consists of a series of numbers on the left of the page, which follow a logical sequence. You are required to choose the next number in the series from the five options on the right. Indicate your answer by filling in completely the appropriate circles on the answer sheet. *Do not use a calculator.*

Time guideline: See how many questions you can answer in 5 minutes. Remember to work accurately as well as quickly.

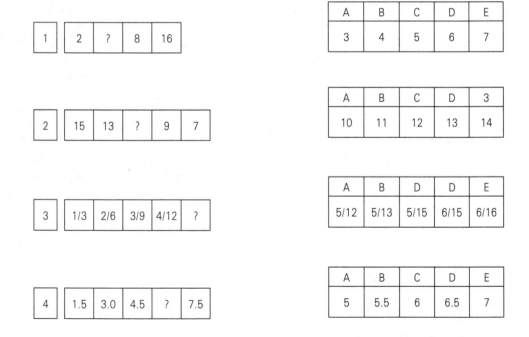

1	2	?	8	16

A	B	C	D	E
3	4	5	6	7

2	15	13	?	9	7

A	B	C	D	3
10	11	12	13	14

3	1/3	2/6	3/9	4/12	?

A	B	D	D	E
5/12	5/13	5/15	6/15	6/16

4	1.5	3.0	4.5	?	7.5

A	B	C	D	E
5	5.5	6	6.5	7

| 5 | 3 | 4 | 5 | 7 | ? |

A	B	C	D	E
9	10	11	12	13

| 6 | ? | 14 | 12 | 11 | 11 |

A	B	C	D	E
13	15	16	17	28

| 7 | 4 | 10 | 18 | ? | 40 |

A	B	C	D	E
28	30	32	34	36

| 8 | 2 | 4 | 8 | 10 | 20 | ? |

A	B	C	D	E
22	24	28	36	40

| 9 | 2 | 3 | 5 | 8 | ? | 21 |

A	B	C	D	E
9	11	13	15	17

| 10 | 2 | 3 | 1 | 4 | 0 | 5 | ? |

A	B	C	D	E
−1	0	1	2	3

Test 12 Answer Sheet

	A	B	C	D	E
1	Ⓐ	Ⓑ	Ⓒ	Ⓓ	Ⓔ
2	Ⓐ	Ⓑ	Ⓒ	Ⓓ	Ⓔ
3	Ⓐ	Ⓑ	Ⓒ	Ⓓ	Ⓔ
4	Ⓐ	Ⓑ	Ⓒ	Ⓓ	Ⓔ
5	Ⓐ	Ⓑ	Ⓒ	Ⓓ	Ⓔ
6	Ⓐ	Ⓑ	Ⓒ	Ⓓ	Ⓔ
7	Ⓐ	Ⓑ	Ⓒ	Ⓓ	Ⓔ
8	Ⓐ	Ⓑ	Ⓒ	Ⓓ	Ⓔ
9	Ⓐ	Ⓑ	Ⓒ	Ⓓ	Ⓔ
10	Ⓐ	Ⓑ	Ⓒ	Ⓓ	Ⓔ

Test 13 Numerical Estimation

In this test your ability to quickly *estimate* the answer to a calculation is being assessed. When you take a test of this type, you will not have sufficient time to calculate the exact answer. This skill is very useful in the automated office environment where calculations made by computers often need to be cross-checked in case of errors in data input.

This type of test is often used in the selection of school leavers and work-experienced applicants, at both clerical and supervisory level, and by a variety of organisations including building societies, banks, retailers and many public sector organisations. Types of job include accounts clerks, clerical supervisors, mail order clerks and positions where VDUs or automated equipment will be used.

Instructions: In this test you are required to *estimate* the order of magnitude of the solution to each calculation and then choose the answer which is nearest to your estimate from the 5 alternative answers.

Indicate your answers by filling in completely the appropriate boxes on the answer sheet. *Do not use a calculator.*

Time guideline: There is no official time guideline for this practice test. However, because in a real live test situation you will not be given sufficient time to calculate the exact answer, work as quickly as you possibly can.

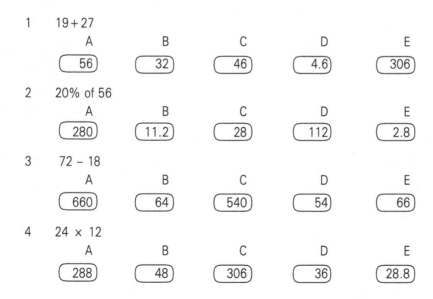

1   19 + 27

A	B	C	D	E
56	32	46	4.6	306

2   20% of 56

A	B	C	D	E
280	11.2	28	112	2.8

3   72 – 18

A	B	C	D	E
660	64	540	54	66

4   24 × 12

A	B	C	D	E
288	48	306	36	28.8

Test 13 Answer Sheet

1   Ⓐ   Ⓑ   Ⓒ   Ⓓ   Ⓔ
2   Ⓐ   Ⓑ   Ⓒ   Ⓓ   Ⓔ
3   Ⓐ   Ⓑ   Ⓒ   Ⓓ   Ⓔ
4   Ⓐ   Ⓑ   Ⓒ   Ⓓ   Ⓔ

Test 14 Numerical Estimation

Now try another numerical estimation test. It also measures your ability to quickly estimate the answers to numerical calculations.

This type of test is often used in the selection of qualified school leavers for modern apprenticeship schemes, or for graduates and work-experienced personnel moving into applied technology areas. It can be used to select candidates for jobs such as electronics and electrical technicians, research technicians and many other technically orientated jobs.

Instructions: This test is a short one with only two questions. As in the previous test, you must *estimate* the answers, and then choose the answer which is nearest to your estimate from the 5 alternative answers. You will be discouraged from making precise calculations by a time constraint.

Indicate your answers by filling in completely the appropriate circles on the answer sheet. *Do not use a calculator.*

Time guideline: There is no official time guideline for this practice test. However, because in a real live test situation you will not be given sufficient time to calculate the exact answer, work as quickly as you possibly can.

1	24 × 0.8 = ?		A	B	C	D	E
			16	220	19	24	140

2	76% of 156 = ?		A	B	C	D	E
			120	160	140	100	180

Test 14 Answer Sheet

	A	B	C	D	E
1	Ⓐ	Ⓑ	Ⓒ	Ⓓ	Ⓔ
2	Ⓐ	Ⓑ	Ⓒ	Ⓓ	Ⓔ

Test 15 Interpreting Data

This test measures your ability to understand facts and figures in statistical tables and make logical deductions from the given information. Certainly, the ability to interpret data from a variety of different sources such as tables, graphs and charts is a common requirement in many managerial and professional jobs.

This type of test is often used to select candidates for administrative and supervisory jobs, as well as junior managers and management trainees, and any job involving analysis or decision-making based on numerical facts.

Instructions: For each question, indicate your answer by filling in completely the appropriate circle on the answer sheet. *Do not use a calculator. You may use rough paper for your workings-out.*

Time guideline: There is no official time guideline for this practice test, however, try to work through the questions as quickly as you can. Remember that accuracy is equally important.

Newspaper Readership				
	Readership (millions)		Percentage of Adults Reading each Paper in 1990	
Daily Newspapers	1981	1990	Males	Females
The Daily Chronicle	3.6	2.9	7	6
Daily News	13.8	9.3	24	18
The Tribune	1.1	1.4	4	3
The Herald	8.5	12.7	30	23
Daily Echo	4.8	4.9	10	12

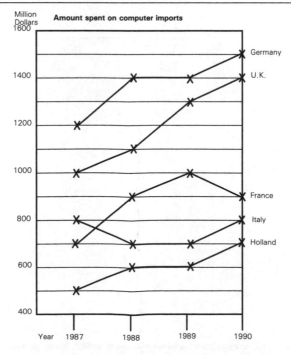

Interpreting Data – Questions

1 Which newspaper was read by a higher percentage of females than males in 1990?

A	B	C	D	E
The Tribune	The Herald	Daily News	Daily Echo	The Daily Chronicle

2 In 1989, how much more than Italy did Germany spend on computer imports?

A	B	C	D	E
650 million	700 million	750 million	800 million	850 million

3 What was the combined readership of the Daily Chronicle, Echo and Tribune in 1981?

A	B	C	D	E
10.6	8.4	9.5	12.2	7.8

4 If the amount spent on computer imports into the U.K. in 1991 was 20% lower than in 1990, what was spent in 1991?

A	B	C	D	E
1080	1120	1160	1220	1300

5 Which newspaper showed the largest change in female readership between 1981 and 1990?

A	B	C	D	E
Daily Echo	The Tribune	The Herald	The Daily Chronicle	Cannot Say

6 Which countries experienced a drop in the value of computers imported from one year to the next?

A	B	C	D	E
France & Italy	France & Holland	Holland & Italy	U.K. & Holland	Italy & U.K.

Test 15 Answer Sheet

	A	B	C	D	E
1	Ⓐ	Ⓑ	Ⓒ	Ⓓ	Ⓔ
2	Ⓐ	Ⓑ	Ⓒ	Ⓓ	Ⓔ
3	Ⓐ	Ⓑ	Ⓒ	Ⓓ	Ⓔ
4	Ⓐ	Ⓑ	Ⓒ	Ⓓ	Ⓔ
5	Ⓐ	Ⓑ	Ⓒ	Ⓓ	Ⓔ
6	Ⓐ	Ⓑ	Ⓒ	Ⓓ	Ⓔ

Answers to numerical reasoning questions

Test 8 Numerical Computation

	A	B	C	D	E
1	Ⓐ	Ⓑ	Ⓒ	●	Ⓔ
2	●	Ⓑ	Ⓒ	Ⓓ	Ⓔ
3	Ⓐ	Ⓑ	●	Ⓓ	Ⓔ
4	Ⓐ	Ⓑ	Ⓒ	Ⓓ	●
5	Ⓐ	Ⓑ	●	Ⓓ	Ⓔ
6	Ⓐ	●	Ⓒ	Ⓓ	Ⓔ
7	●	Ⓑ	Ⓒ	Ⓓ	Ⓔ
8	Ⓐ	●	Ⓒ	Ⓓ	Ⓔ
9	Ⓐ	Ⓑ	Ⓒ	●	Ⓔ
10	Ⓐ	Ⓑ	Ⓒ	●	Ⓔ

Test 9 Numerical Computation

	A	B	C	D	E
1	Ⓐ	●	Ⓒ	Ⓓ	Ⓔ
2	Ⓐ	Ⓑ	●	Ⓓ	Ⓔ
3	Ⓐ	Ⓑ	Ⓒ	Ⓓ	●
4	Ⓐ	Ⓑ	Ⓒ	●	Ⓔ
5	Ⓐ	Ⓑ	●	Ⓓ	Ⓔ
6	Ⓐ	Ⓑ	Ⓒ	●	Ⓔ
7	Ⓐ	Ⓑ	Ⓒ	Ⓓ	●
8	●	Ⓑ	Ⓒ	Ⓓ	Ⓔ
9	Ⓐ	Ⓑ	Ⓒ	Ⓓ	●

Test 10 Numerical Reasoning

	A	B	C	D	E
1	Ⓐ	Ⓑ	Ⓒ	Ⓓ	●
2	Ⓐ	●	Ⓒ	Ⓓ	Ⓔ
3	Ⓐ	●	Ⓒ	Ⓓ	Ⓔ
4	Ⓐ	Ⓑ	Ⓒ	Ⓓ	●
5	●	Ⓑ	Ⓒ	Ⓓ	Ⓔ
6	Ⓐ	Ⓑ	Ⓒ	●	Ⓔ
7	Ⓐ	Ⓑ	●	Ⓓ	Ⓔ
8	Ⓐ	Ⓑ	Ⓒ	●	Ⓔ

Test 11 Numerical Reasoning

	A	B	C	D	E
1	Ⓐ	●	Ⓒ	Ⓓ	Ⓔ
2	Ⓐ	Ⓑ	●	Ⓓ	Ⓔ
3	Ⓐ	Ⓑ	●	Ⓓ	Ⓔ
4	Ⓐ	Ⓑ	Ⓒ	●	Ⓔ
5	●	Ⓑ	Ⓒ	Ⓓ	Ⓔ
6	Ⓐ	Ⓑ	Ⓒ	Ⓓ	●

Test 12 Number Series

	A	B	C	D	E
1	Ⓐ	●	Ⓒ	Ⓓ	Ⓔ
2	Ⓐ	●	Ⓒ	Ⓓ	Ⓔ
3	Ⓐ	Ⓑ	●	Ⓓ	Ⓔ
4	Ⓐ	Ⓑ	●	Ⓓ	Ⓔ
5	●	Ⓑ	Ⓒ	Ⓓ	Ⓔ
6	Ⓐ	Ⓑ	Ⓒ	●	Ⓔ
7	●	Ⓑ	Ⓒ	Ⓓ	Ⓔ
8	●	Ⓑ	Ⓒ	Ⓓ	Ⓔ
9	Ⓐ	Ⓑ	●	Ⓓ	Ⓔ
10	●	Ⓑ	Ⓒ	Ⓓ	Ⓔ

Test 13 Numerical Estimation

	A	B	C	D	E
1	Ⓐ	Ⓑ	●	Ⓓ	Ⓔ
2	Ⓐ	●	Ⓒ	Ⓓ	Ⓔ
3	Ⓐ	Ⓑ	Ⓒ	●	Ⓔ
4	●	Ⓑ	Ⓒ	Ⓓ	Ⓔ

Test 14 Numerical Estimation

	A	B	C	D	E
1	Ⓐ	Ⓑ	●	Ⓓ	Ⓔ
2	●	Ⓑ	Ⓒ	Ⓓ	Ⓔ

Test 15 Interpreting Data

	A	B	C	D	E
1	Ⓐ	Ⓑ	Ⓒ	●	Ⓔ
2	Ⓐ	●	Ⓒ	Ⓓ	Ⓔ
3	Ⓐ	Ⓑ	●	Ⓓ	Ⓔ
4	Ⓐ	●	Ⓒ	Ⓓ	Ⓔ
5	Ⓐ	Ⓑ	Ⓒ	Ⓓ	●
6	●	Ⓑ	Ⓒ	Ⓓ	Ⓔ

How to improve your performance

However numerical reasoning questions are presented you really do need a sound understanding of the following basic maths skills:

✓ addition
✓ subtraction
✓ multiplication
✓ division
✓ decimal numbers
✓ fractions
✓ percentages

This is essential, especially for questions which require any sort of mental calculation. Psychometric tests which measure basic mathematical ability are becoming more and more common.

Remember that for many numerical reasoning tests, the use of a calculator is prohibited (however, take along a calculator, just in case).

Basic maths skills are all very well, but often your ability to *reason* with numbers is also being tested. Here are some ways to improve your numerical reasoning ability:

◆ Practice simple maths with or without a calculator.
◆ Do number puzzles in newspapers and magazines.
◆ Do the scoring when playing games like darts, card games, etc.
◆ Calculate how much your shopping will cost before you reach the till.
◆ Work out how much change you should receive when you pay for something.
◆ Learn your times tables off by heart.
◆ Read financial reports in newspapers.
◆ Study tables of data.

CHAPTER SIX

Abstract Reasoning

Abstract reasoning tests, or diagrammatic reasoning tests as they are sometimes called, are psychometric tests which use diagrams, symbols, signs or shapes instead of words and numbers. In other words, they are *visual* questions. And because they require good visual-thinking skills rather than verbal or numerical skills, they are often considered to be a very good indicator of a person's general intellectual ability. For this reason they are given to applicants over a wide range of jobs.

All abstract reasoning tests are strictly timed, and *each question will have one, and only one correct answer.*

In this chapter

In this chapter there are four different abstract reasoning tests for you to try. Before each one I've indicated for what sort of job (and at what level) you might be expected to take that particular type of test.

At the end of this chapter there is a section entitled **How to improve your performance** which is intended to help you do just that across the whole range of abstract reasoning tests. Included in this section are some hints on tackling the questions themselves. If you have a problem with any of the questions then hopefully the advice contained in this section will get you back on track. Remember, however, that all of us have strengths and weaknesses, and everyone will have some difficulty with some of the tests in this book.

Test 16 Diagrammatic Series

The following test measures your ability to recognise logical sequences within a series of diagrams or symbols.

This type of test is often used to assess reasoning skills at administrative, supervisory and junior management levels – in fact any occupation where logical or analytical reasoning is required. It could be used to select applicants for administrative and supervisory jobs, junior managers, management trainees, jobs involving technical research and also computer programming.

Instructions: Each problem in the test consists of a series of diagrams, on the left of the page, which follow a logical sequence. You are required to choose the next diagram in the series from the five options on the right. Indicate your answer by filling in completely the appropriate circle on the answer sheet.

Time guideline: See how many questions you can answer in 5 minutes. Remember to work accurately as well as quickly.

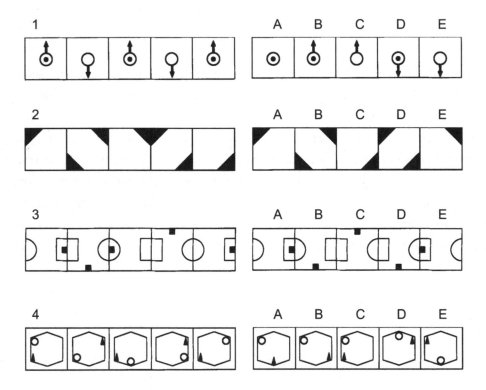

Test 16 © SHL Group Plc 2001. SHL and OPQ are registered trademarks of SHL Group plc which are registered in the United Kingdom and other countries.

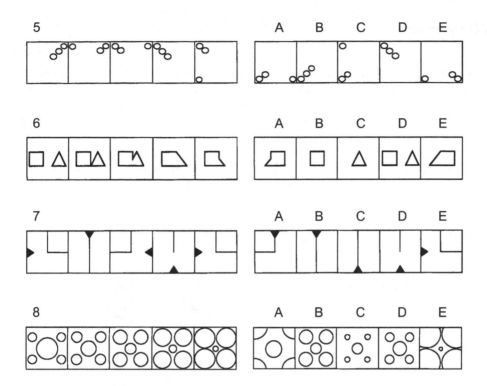

Test 16 Answer Sheet

	A	B	C	D	E
1	Ⓐ	Ⓑ	Ⓒ	Ⓓ	Ⓔ
2	Ⓐ	Ⓑ	Ⓒ	Ⓓ	Ⓔ
3	Ⓐ	Ⓑ	Ⓒ	Ⓓ	Ⓔ
4	Ⓐ	Ⓑ	Ⓒ	Ⓓ	Ⓔ
5	Ⓐ	Ⓑ	Ⓒ	Ⓓ	Ⓔ
6	Ⓐ	Ⓑ	Ⓒ	Ⓓ	Ⓔ
7	Ⓐ	Ⓑ	Ⓒ	Ⓓ	Ⓔ
8	Ⓐ	Ⓑ	Ⓒ	Ⓓ	Ⓔ

Test 17 Diagramming

This abstract reasoning test measures logical analysis through the ability to follow complex instructions. It simulates the ability to handle multiple and independent commands, an important ability in most IT jobs. This type of test is therefore specifically designed for the selection, development and promotion of staff working in the IT industry, for example, software engineers, systems analysts, programmers and database administrators.

Instructions: In this test, figures (shapes) in BOXES are presented in columns. They are changed in various ways by commands represented as symbols in CIRCLES. A complete list of these commands and what they do is shown below.

Time guideline: See how many questions you can answer in 4 minutes.

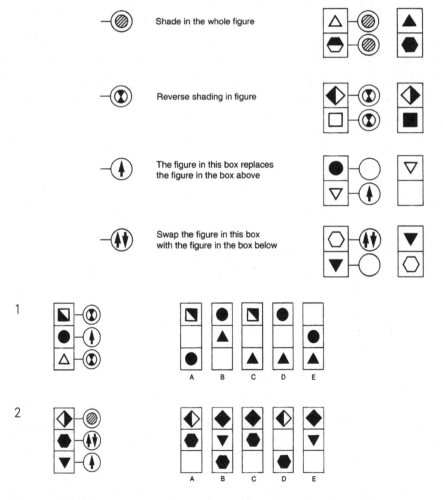

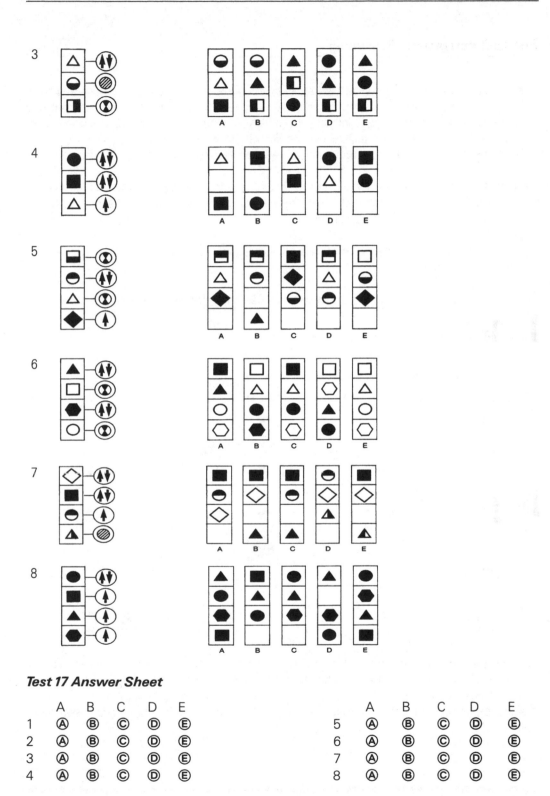

	A	B	C	D	E
1	Ⓐ	Ⓑ	Ⓒ	Ⓓ	Ⓔ
2	Ⓐ	Ⓑ	Ⓒ	Ⓓ	Ⓔ
3	Ⓐ	Ⓑ	Ⓒ	Ⓓ	Ⓔ
4	Ⓐ	Ⓑ	Ⓒ	Ⓓ	Ⓔ

	A	B	C	D	E
5	Ⓐ	Ⓑ	Ⓒ	Ⓓ	Ⓔ
6	Ⓐ	Ⓑ	Ⓒ	Ⓓ	Ⓔ
7	Ⓐ	Ⓑ	Ⓒ	Ⓓ	Ⓔ
8	Ⓐ	Ⓑ	Ⓒ	Ⓓ	Ⓔ

Test 18 Diagrammatic Reasoning

This abstract reasoning test measures your ability to infer a set of rules from a flow-chart, and apply these rules to new situations, and is specifically designed for the selection, development and promotion of staff working in the IT industry. It is a high-level measure of symbolic reasoning ability and is specially relevant in jobs that require the capacity to work through complex problems in a systematic and analytical manner, for example, in systems analysis and programming design.

Instructions: In this test you are shown a number of diagrams in which figures (shapes) in BOXES are altered by rules shown as symbols in CIRCLES. The rules can alter each figure by changing its colour, its size, its shape or by turning it upside down.

Paths through each diagram are shown as black or white arrows. You must follow paths which include only one type of arrow.

Work out what each rule does and then answer the questions below each diagram.

Time guideline: See how many questions you can answer in 4 minutes.

Look at the example below:

DIAGRAM

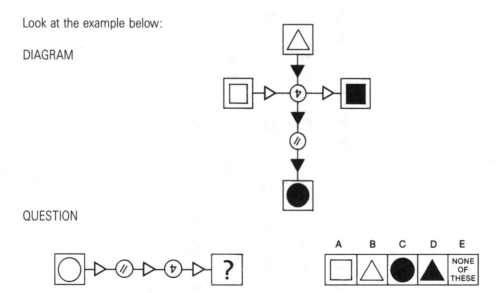

QUESTION

In the diagram, working horizontally, the white square becomes a black square so ⊽ must be a colour changing rule. Working vertically, the white triangle becomes a black circle. Since we know that ⊽ changes the colour of a figure, // must be a shape-changing rule. Applying these rules to the question, it is possible to identify that the white circle becomes a black triangle, so D is the correct answer to the question.

DIAGRAM

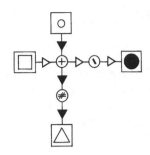

1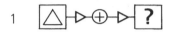

2

3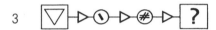

DIAGRAM

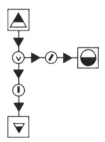

4

5

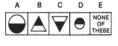

6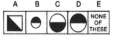

Test 18 Answer Sheet

	A	B	C	D	E			A	B	C	D	E
1	Ⓐ	Ⓑ	Ⓒ	Ⓓ	Ⓔ		4	Ⓐ	Ⓑ	Ⓒ	Ⓓ	Ⓔ
2	Ⓐ	Ⓑ	Ⓒ	Ⓓ	Ⓔ		5	Ⓐ	Ⓑ	Ⓒ	Ⓓ	Ⓔ
3	Ⓐ	Ⓑ	Ⓒ	Ⓓ	Ⓔ		6	Ⓐ	Ⓑ	Ⓒ	Ⓓ	Ⓔ

Test 19 Diagrammatic Thinking

The following test measures your ability to apply checks and follow a sequence of symbols arranged in a logical order. This type of test is often used in the selection of qualified school leavers for modern apprenticeship schemes and other technically orientated jobs.

It is also used to select graduates applying to work in applied technical areas, for example, electronics technicians, electrical technicians, research technicians and also for jobs tracking process control systems, debugging software and systems design.

Instructions: In this test you are required to follow the progress of a 'Development figure' which is changed according to instructions contained in a series of 'Process boxes'. These boxes are divided into three levels, each of which affects the development figure in a given way.

Time guideline: There is no official time guideline for this practice test, however, try to work through the questions as quickly as you can. Remember that accuracy is equally important as speed.

Process box		
Level 1	X	means change SHAPE from circle to square or vice versa
Level 2	X	means change SIZE from large to small or vice versa
Level 3	X	means change COLOUR from black to white or vice versa

NB: The absence of a cross means no change to that aspect of the figure.

Your task is to identify which process needs to be repeated at the end of the series in order to achieve the required 'Target' figure. Indicate your answer by fully blackening the appropriate circles A, B, C or D on Answer Sheet 19.

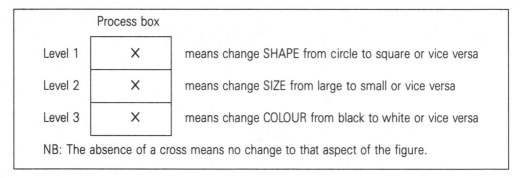

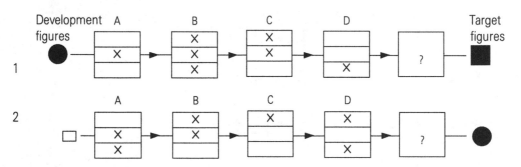

Test 19 Answer Sheet

	A	B	C	D
1	Ⓐ	Ⓑ	Ⓒ	Ⓓ
2	Ⓐ	Ⓑ	Ⓒ	Ⓓ

Answers to abstract reasoning questions

Test 16 Diagrammatic Series

	A	B	C	D	E
1	Ⓐ	Ⓑ	Ⓒ	Ⓓ	●
2	Ⓐ	●	Ⓒ	Ⓓ	Ⓔ
3	Ⓐ	Ⓑ	Ⓒ	●	Ⓔ
4	Ⓐ	Ⓑ	Ⓒ	●	Ⓔ
5	Ⓐ	Ⓑ	●	Ⓓ	Ⓔ
6	Ⓐ	●	Ⓒ	Ⓓ	Ⓔ
7	Ⓐ	●	Ⓒ	Ⓓ	Ⓔ
8	Ⓐ	Ⓑ	Ⓒ	Ⓓ	●

Test 17 Diagramming

	A	B	C	D	E
1	Ⓐ	Ⓑ	Ⓒ	●	Ⓔ
2	Ⓐ	Ⓑ	●	Ⓓ	Ⓔ
3	Ⓐ	●	Ⓒ	Ⓓ	Ⓔ
4	Ⓐ	Ⓑ	Ⓒ	Ⓓ	●
5	●	Ⓑ	Ⓒ	Ⓓ	Ⓔ
6	Ⓐ	Ⓑ	Ⓒ	Ⓓ	●
7	Ⓐ	●	Ⓒ	Ⓓ	Ⓔ
8	Ⓐ	Ⓑ	●	Ⓓ	Ⓔ

Test 18 Diagrammatic Reasoning

	A	B	C	D	E
1	Ⓐ	●	Ⓒ	Ⓓ	Ⓔ
2	Ⓐ	Ⓑ	●	Ⓓ	Ⓔ
3	Ⓐ	Ⓑ	Ⓒ	●	Ⓔ
4	●	Ⓑ	Ⓒ	Ⓓ	Ⓔ
5	Ⓐ	Ⓑ	Ⓒ	●	Ⓔ
6	Ⓐ	Ⓑ	Ⓒ	Ⓓ	●

Test 19 Diagrammatic Thinking

	A	B	C	D
1	Ⓐ	Ⓑ	●	Ⓓ
2	●	Ⓑ	Ⓒ	Ⓓ

How to improve your performance

◆ Try doing puzzles in newspapers, magazines and quiz books which involve diagrams.

◆ Play games which involve thinking out a problem visually and in a logical sequence, for example chess, Labyrinth, or computer Freecell.

◆ Abstract reasoning questions are often presented as sequences. Watch out for sequences which have separate components which work in different ways.

◆ At first glance, abstract reasoning questions may seem impossible. But by reading the instructions very carefully, and possibly by having a look at the answers to the first few questions, you'll see they are not so difficult after all.

CHAPTER SEVEN

Spatial Reasoning

There are people who may not be so hot with words or numbers, but are good with space. They can see an object in their mind, and manipulate it, turn it round, upside down, or pull it in and out of shape. These people are said to have good spatial awareness, and they often find success in the field of design, illustration, architecture, publishing, technology, electronic engineering and IT. Therefore it is hardly surprising to find employers in these industries using spatial reasoning tests to select applicants for jobs which require three-dimensional perception.

The interesting thing about these test questions is that people with extremely good spatial awareness 'see' the solution immediately, without having to even think about it. But for most of us, the answers are not so obvious and you might need to make more of an effort to manipulate the shapes in your mind (or even do as I do – physically turn the page round).

In common with other psychometric tests, spatial reasoning tests are strictly timed, and *each question has one, and only one correct answer*.

In this chapter

In this chapter there are three different spatial reasoning psychometric tests for you to try. Before each one I've indicated for what sort of job (and at what level) you might be expected to take that particular type of test.

At the end of this chapter there is a section entitled **How to improve your performance** which is intended to help you do just that. Included in this section are some hints on tackling the questions themselves. If you have a problem with any of the questions then hopefully the advice contained in this section will get you back on track. Remember, however, that all of us have strengths and weaknesses, and everyone will have some difficulty with some of the tests in this book.

Test 20 Spatial Recognition

The following test measures your ability to recognise shapes in two dimensions. This type of test is often used in the selection and development of personnel in technically or practically orientated jobs, for example, apprentice fitters, mechanics and constructions workers.

Instructions: In this test you are to choose the shape on the right which is identical to the given shape. The identical shape may be rotated on the page but not turned over. Indicate your answers by filling in completely the appropriate circles on the answer sheet.

Time guideline: See how many questions you can answer in 2 minutes. Remember to work accurately as well as quickly.

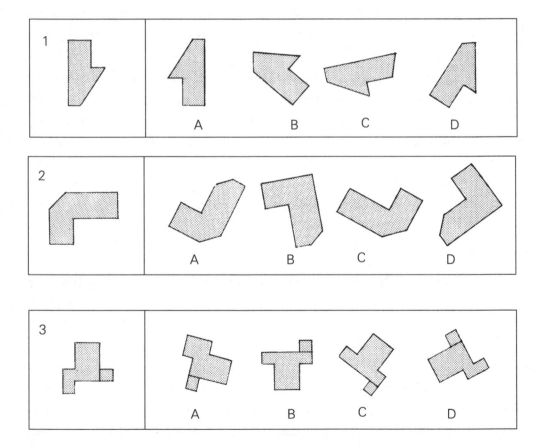

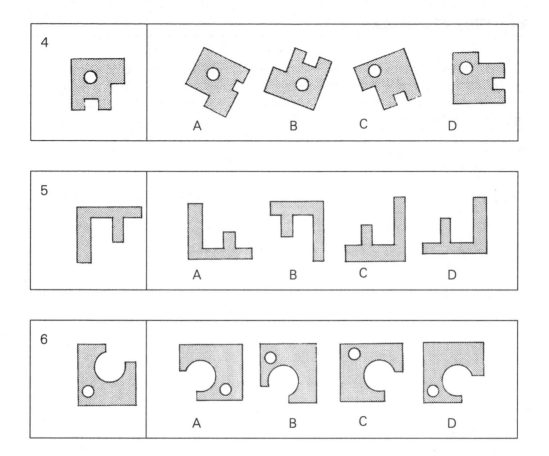

Test 20 Answer Sheet

	A	B	C	D
1	Ⓐ	Ⓑ	Ⓒ	Ⓓ
2	Ⓐ	Ⓑ	Ⓒ	Ⓓ
3	Ⓐ	Ⓑ	Ⓒ	Ⓓ
4	Ⓐ	Ⓑ	Ⓒ	Ⓓ
5	Ⓐ	Ⓑ	Ⓒ	Ⓓ
6	Ⓐ	Ⓑ	Ⓒ	Ⓓ

Test 21 Visual Estimation

The following test measures spatial perception and the ability to make accurate visual comparisons. This type of test is often used in the selection and development of personnel in technically or practically orientated jobs, and is particularly suitable for craft and operator level jobs involving basic design and assembly work.

Instructions: In this test you are to choose the two shapes which are identical and fill in the appropriate *two* circles on the answer sheet.

Time guideline: See how many questions you can answer in 2 minutes. Remember to work accurately as well as quickly.

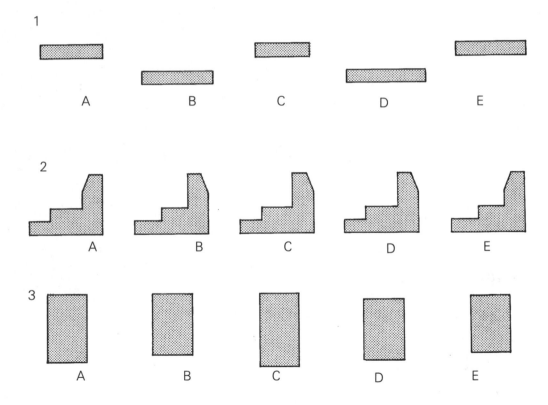

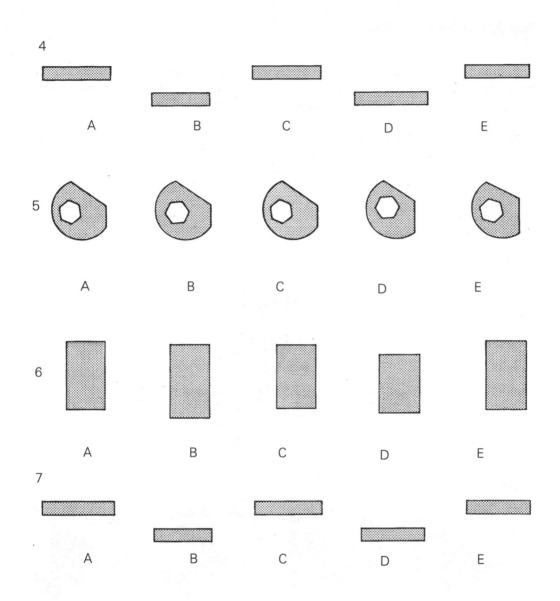

4

    A   B   C   D   E

5

    A   B   C   D   E

6

    A   B   C   D   E

7

    A   B   C   D   E

Test 21 Answer Sheet

	A	B	C	D	E
1	Ⓐ	Ⓑ	Ⓒ	Ⓓ	Ⓔ
2	Ⓐ	Ⓑ	Ⓒ	Ⓓ	Ⓔ
3	Ⓐ	Ⓑ	Ⓒ	Ⓓ	Ⓔ
4	Ⓐ	Ⓑ	Ⓒ	Ⓓ	Ⓔ
5	Ⓐ	Ⓑ	Ⓒ	Ⓓ	Ⓔ
6	Ⓐ	Ⓑ	Ⓒ	Ⓓ	Ⓔ
7	Ⓐ	Ⓑ	Ⓒ	Ⓓ	Ⓔ

Test 22 Spatial Reasoning

The following test measures your ability to visualise and manipulate shapes in three dimensions given a two-dimensional drawing. The test is high level, and could be used to select engineers, designers, draughts people and IT staff working with graphics or CAD/CAM software.

Instructions: In this test you are given a pattern which, if cut out, could be folded to make a three-dimensional shape (a box). You must decide which, if any, of the four boxes could be made by folding the pattern, and indicate this by filling in completely the appropriate circle on the answer sheet. If you think that none of the boxes could be made from the pattern, fill in circle 'E' on the answer sheet.

Time guideline: See how many questions you can answer in 3 minutes. Remember to work accurately as well as quickly.

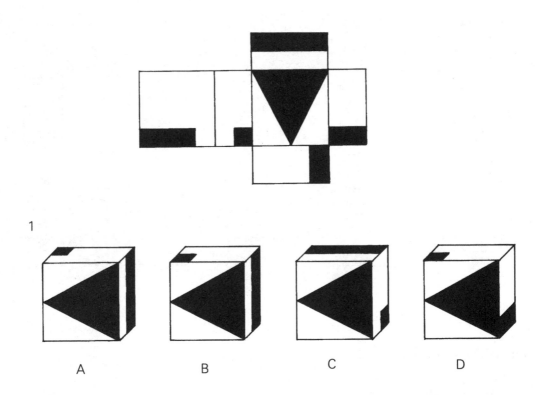

1

A   B   C   D

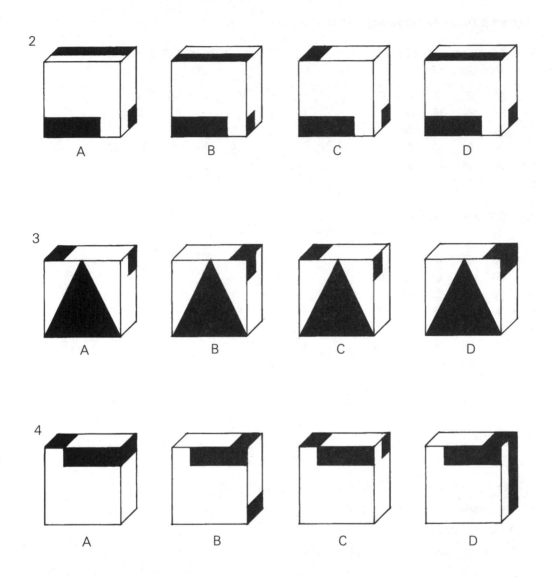

Test 22 Answer Sheet

	A	B	C	D	E
1	Ⓐ	Ⓑ	Ⓒ	Ⓓ	Ⓔ
2	Ⓐ	Ⓑ	Ⓒ	Ⓓ	Ⓔ
3	Ⓐ	Ⓑ	Ⓒ	Ⓓ	Ⓔ
4	Ⓐ	Ⓑ	Ⓒ	Ⓓ	Ⓔ

Answers to spatial reasoning questions

Test 20 Spatial Recognition

	A	B	C	D
1	●	B	C	D
2	A	B	●	D
3	A	B	C	●
4	A	●	C	D
5	A	B	C	●
6	A	B	●	D

Test 22 Spatial Reasoning

	A	B	C	D	E
1	A	●	C	D	E
2	A	B	C	●	E
3	A	B	●	D	E
4	A	B	C	D	●

Test 21 Visual Estimation

	A	B	C	D	E
1	A	●	C	D	●
2	A	B	●	●	E
3	A	●	C	●	E
4	●	B	●	D	E
5	●	B	●	D	E
6	●	B	C	D	●
7	A	B	C	●	●

How to improve your performance

- Look at plans and DIY manuals.
- Do jigsaw puzzles and play chess.
- Assemble construction sets.
- Make up plans, patterns and designs.
- Make up simple patterns and try to visualise what they would look like when rotated or flipped over.
- Imagine how various objects look from different angles.
- Try to break down puzzles into chunks.
- Try drawing out the shapes in these tests on a sheet of paper. Actually handling the shapes and physically turning them round (or turning the book round) can help you understand how the 'puzzles' work.
- Try to get as much practice as you can.

CHAPTER EIGHT

Mechanical Comprehension

Mechanical comprehension tests are written, multiple-choice psychometric tests which are used as part of the selection procedure for technically or practically orientated jobs. They test your understanding of how mechanical and technical things work.

To a certain extent, you either have this ability or you don't. If you can answer the test questions in this chapter easily, you're probably a very practical person and always have been. If, on the other hand, you're like me and are incapable of even programming the DVD, it's unlikely that you'll be applying for a job in engineering or mechanics anyway.

But for those of you who are quite capable of taking your car to pieces and putting the bits back in the right places, I have included two mechanical comprehension tests for you to try.

As with other psychometric tests, mechanical comprehension tests are strictly timed, and *each question will have one, and only one correct answer.*

In this chapter

In this chapter there are two mechanical comprehension tests for you to try. Before each test I have indicated for what sort of job (and at what level) you might be expected to take that particular type of test.

At the end of this chapter there is a section entitled **How to improve your performance** which is intended to help you do just that. Included in this section are some hints on tackling the questions themselves. If you have a problem with any of the questions then hopefully the advice contained in this section will get you back on track. Remember, however, that all of us have strengths and weaknesses, and everyone will have some difficulty with some of the tests in this book.

Test 23 Mechanical Comprehension

This test assesses your understanding of basic mechanical principles and their application to such devices as pulleys and gears and simple structures.

This type of test is often used in the selection and development of individuals in technically or practically orientated jobs such as craft apprentices, technical apprentices, skilled operatives and technical supervisors and in engineering and mechanics.

Instructions: Each problem in the test consists of a question which refers to a drawing. Choose the best answer to each question, indicating your answer by filling in completely the appropriate circle on the answer sheet.

Time guideline: There are 4 questions – see how many you can do in 2 minutes.

1   With which spanner will it be easier to undo the nut?

    If equal, mark C.

2   Which shelf will support the heaviest load?

3   In which direction can pulley-wheel 'X' turn?

If it cannot turn, mark C.

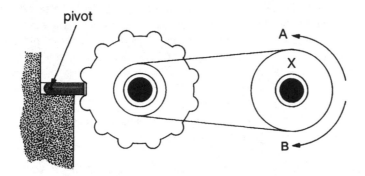

4   Which way will the pointer move when the shaft turns in the direction of the arrow?

If neither, mark C.

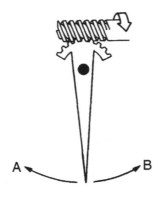

Test 23 Answer Sheet

	A	B	C
1	Ⓐ	Ⓑ	Ⓒ
2	Ⓐ	Ⓑ	Ⓒ
3	Ⓐ	Ⓑ	Ⓒ
4	Ⓐ	Ⓑ	Ⓒ

Test 24 Mechanical Comprehension

This test assesses your understanding of basic mechanical principles and their application to such devices as pulleys and gears and simple structures.

This type of test is often used in the selection and development of individuals in technically or practically orientated jobs. It could be used to recruit qualified school leavers into modern craft and technical apprenticeships, or for graduates or work experienced personnel moving into applied technology areas and jobs such as process control operators and electrical or research technicians, and in engineering and mechanics.

Instructions: The test is based on mechanical principles. Each problem in the test consists of a question which refers to a drawing. Choose the best answer to each question, indicating your answer by filling in completely the appropriate circle on the answer sheet.

Time guideline: There is no official time guideline for this practice test, however, try to work through the questions as quickly as you can.

1   Which screw is more likely to pull out of the wall when a load is applied to the hook?

If equally likely, mark C.

2   Which apparatus requires less force to begin moving the block?

If equal, mark C.

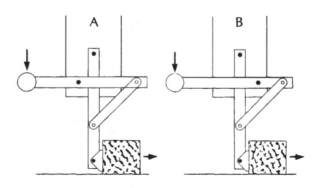

Test 24 Answer Sheet

	A	B	C
1	Ⓐ	Ⓑ	Ⓒ
2	Ⓐ	Ⓑ	Ⓒ

Answers to mechanical comprehension questions

Test 23 Mechanical Comprehension

	A	B	C
1	●	Ⓑ	Ⓒ
2	Ⓐ	Ⓑ	●
3	Ⓐ	●	Ⓒ
4	Ⓐ	●	Ⓒ

Test 24 Mechanical Comprehension

	A	B	C
1	●	Ⓑ	Ⓒ
2	Ⓐ	●	Ⓒ

How to improve your performance

- ◆ Attempt lots of DIY.
- ◆ Try to understand how household objects work.
- ◆ Repair mechanical things, for example, a vacuum cleaner or a door lock.
- ◆ Take things to pieces and then reassemble them.
- ◆ Play with technical or construction sets.
- ◆ Build working models.
- ◆ Looking at the answers to the questions should give you a better understanding of the underlying mechanical principles involved.

CHAPTER NINE

Fault Diagnosis

Fault diagnosis tests are written, multiple-choice psychometric tests which are used as part of the selection procedure for technically or practically orientated jobs.

They assess your ability to identify faults in logical systems – an important skill which has many applications including those of electronics fault finding, debugging of software, process control systems and systems design.

As with other psychometric tests, fault diagnosis tests are strictly timed, and *each question will have one, and only one correct answer.*

In this chapter

In this chapter there are two fault diagnosis practice tests for you to try. Before each test I have indicated for what sort of job (and at what level) you might be expected to take that particular type of test.

At the end of this chapter there is a section entitled **How to improve your performance** which is intended to help you do just that. However, remember that all of us have strengths and weaknesses, and everyone will have some difficulty with some of the tests in this book.

Test 25 Fault diagnosis

This test measures your ability to identify faults in systems. This type of test is often used in the selection of individuals in technically or practically orientated jobs such as technical apprentices, skilled operatives, technical supervisors and jobs involving electronics fault finding.

Time guideline: See how many questions you can answer in 3 minutes.

Instructions: You are required to follow sequences made up of a number of switches labelled A, B, C, and D. Each switch, when working properly, has a specified effect on a set of numbered lights (shown in a rectangle on the left). The rectangle on the right contains the result of that sequence.

In each case, **one** of the switches is not working and has no effect on the numbered lights. A list of the switches and what they can do is shown below.

Switch	Effect when working
A	Turns 1 and 2 on/off ie, black to white and vice versa
B	Turns 3 and 4 on/off ie, black to white and vice versa
C	Turns 1 and 3 on/off ie, black to white and vice versa
D	Turns 2 and 4 on/off ie, black to white and vice versa

○ = ON
● = OFF
Remember – a switch not working has no effect

Your task is to identify the switch which is not working in each sequence and indicate this by fully blackening the appropriate circle on Answer Sheet 22.

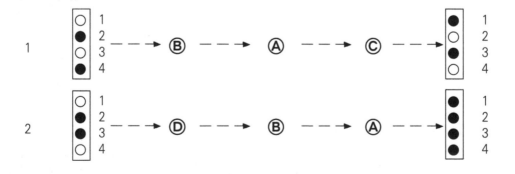

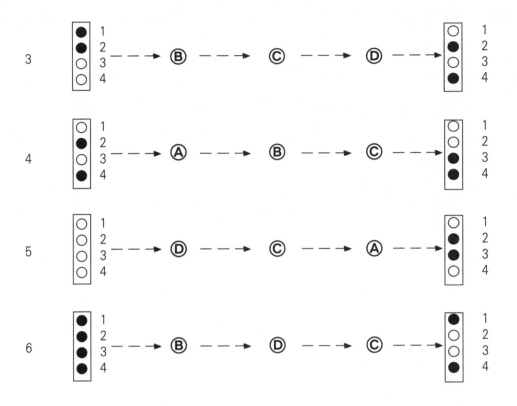

Test 25 Answer Sheet

	A	B	C	D
1	Ⓐ	Ⓑ	Ⓒ	Ⓓ
2	Ⓐ	Ⓑ	Ⓒ	Ⓓ
3	Ⓐ	Ⓑ	Ⓒ	Ⓓ
4	Ⓐ	Ⓑ	Ⓒ	Ⓓ
5	Ⓐ	Ⓑ	Ⓒ	Ⓓ
6	Ⓐ	Ⓑ	Ⓒ	Ⓓ

Test 26 Fault finding

This test measures your ability to identify faults in systems. This type of test is often used in the selection of qualified school leavers for technical apprenticeships, or for graduates or work experienced personnel moving into applied technology areas. Uses include electronics fault finding, debugging of software, process control systems and systems design.

Time guideline: There is no official time guideline for this test. However, try to work through the questions as quickly and as accurately as possible.

Instructions: You are required to follow sequences made up of a number of switches labelled A, B and C. Each switch, when working properly, has a specified effect on a set of numbered lights (shown in a square on the left). The circle on the right contains the result of a particular sequence.

In each case, **one** of the switches is not working and so has no effect on the numbered lights. A list of the switches and what they can do is shown below.

Switch	Effect when working
A	Turns 1 and 3 on/off i.e. from black to white or vice versa
B	Turns 3 and 4 on/off i.e. from black to white or vice versa
C	Turns 2 and 4 on/off i.e. from black to white or vice versa
	Remember – a switch that is not working has no effect

Your task is to identify the switch which is not working and indicate this by fully blackening the appropriate circles A, B or C on Answer Sheet 26.

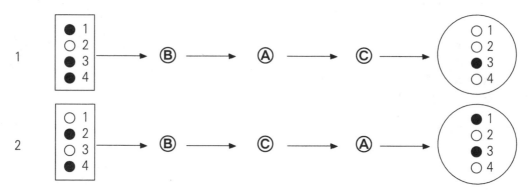

Test 26 Answer Sheet

	A	B	C
1	Ⓐ	Ⓑ	Ⓒ
2	Ⓐ	Ⓑ	Ⓒ

Answers to fault diagnosis questions

Test 25 Fault Diagnosis

	A	B	C	D
1	Ⓐ	Ⓑ	●	Ⓓ
2	Ⓐ	●	Ⓒ	Ⓓ
3	Ⓐ	Ⓑ	Ⓒ	●
4	Ⓐ	●	Ⓒ	Ⓓ
5	Ⓐ	Ⓑ	Ⓒ	●
6	Ⓐ	Ⓑ	●	Ⓓ

Test 26 Fault Finding

	A	B	C
1	Ⓐ	Ⓑ	●
2	Ⓐ	●	Ⓒ

How to improve your performance

◆ Think about the things that can go wrong with a piece of equipment, for example, a car, a washing machine, etc. What effect would any particular fault have? How would you diagnose the fault? What tests would pinpoint where the fault lay?

◆ Learn a programming language: HTML, Basic, C++, Java.

CHAPTER TEN

Accuracy Tests

Tests that measure accuracy have various names. They can be called 'acuity' tests, or 'clerical' tests, but whatever the label they all basically do the same thing. They are multiple choice tests which measure your ability to:

✓ deal with information

✓ follow instructions precisely

✓ work at high speed

✓ check material for errors

✓ maintain a high level of accuracy and concentration.

As with all the different types of psychometric test, tests of accuracy are strictly timed, and *each question will have one, and only one correct answer.*

In this chapter

In this chapter there are six different tests for you to try. Before each one I've indicated for what sort of job (and at what level) you might be expected to take that particular type of test.

At the end of this chapter there is a section entitled **How to improve your performance** which is intended to help you do just that. Included in this section are some hints on tackling the questions themselves. If you have a problem with any of the questions then hopefully the advice contained in this section will get you back on track. However, remember that all of us have strengths and weaknesses, and everyone will have some difficulty with some of the tests in this book.

Test 27 Basic Checking

This test measure speed and accuracy of checking at a basic level. This type of test is often used to select clerical staff whose job includes routine checking.

Instructions: Find the two codes which are the same in each line and mark the letters for the two appropriate columns in the answer section.

Time guideline: There are 14 questions – see how many you can do in 2 minutes.

	A	B	C	D	E
1	6522	5262	6252	6522	6225
2	SSGB	SGSB	SSBG	GBSS	SSBG
3	8553	8535	5852	8535	8355
4	YWHN	YHWN	YWHN	YNWH	NYWH
5	57657	57675	57675	56675	57765
6	ZHHCZ	ZZCHH	ZCHHZ	ZCZHH	ZCHHZ
7	82443	84243	84234	84342	84243
8	LBENI	LEBNI	LIBNE	LBNEI	LBNEI
9	232215	232125	231225	232125	232151
10	JWHRWF	JWHWRF	JWHRWF	JFWHRW	JHWWRF
11	9760207	9760270	9706207	9760027	9760207

12	MUBFBII	MUBFIBI	MUBBFII	MBBUFII	MUBBFII
13	56932099	56923099	56930299	56932099	56392099
14	YBZGOCXF	YBZOGXCF	YBZOGCXF	YBZOGCXF	YZBOGCXF

Test 27 Answer Sheet

	A	B	C	D	E
1	Ⓐ	Ⓑ	Ⓒ	Ⓓ	Ⓔ
2	Ⓐ	Ⓑ	Ⓒ	Ⓓ	Ⓔ
3	Ⓐ	Ⓑ	Ⓒ	Ⓓ	Ⓔ
4	Ⓐ	Ⓑ	Ⓒ	Ⓓ	Ⓔ
5	Ⓐ	Ⓑ	Ⓒ	Ⓓ	Ⓔ
6	Ⓐ	Ⓑ	Ⓒ	Ⓓ	Ⓔ
7	Ⓐ	Ⓑ	Ⓒ	Ⓓ	Ⓔ
8	Ⓐ	Ⓑ	Ⓒ	Ⓓ	Ⓔ
9	Ⓐ	Ⓑ	Ⓒ	Ⓓ	Ⓔ
10	Ⓐ	Ⓑ	Ⓒ	Ⓓ	Ⓔ
11	Ⓐ	Ⓑ	Ⓒ	Ⓓ	Ⓔ
12	Ⓐ	Ⓑ	Ⓒ	Ⓓ	Ⓔ
13	Ⓐ	Ⓑ	Ⓒ	Ⓓ	Ⓔ
14	Ⓐ	Ⓑ	Ⓒ	Ⓓ	Ⓔ

Test 28 Computer Checking

This test measures speed and accuracy in the checking of character strings made up of letters, numbers and symbols. These are important skills in any area of programming and especially important for computer data entry staff. This type of test is designed for applicants with A level to graduate qualifications, or similar.

Instructions: Find the two sets of characters which are the same in each line and mark the letters for the two appropriate columns (A, B, C, D or E) on the answer section.

Time guideline: There are 20 questions – see how many you can do in 3 minutes.

	A	B	C	D	E
1	15*TZ	1*5TZ	15*T2	15*TZ	IS*TZ
2	TVB$	TBV$	TBVS	TB$V	TBV$
3	GS24B	G2S4B	GS24B	GS2B4	GS428
4	LOGGB	LO6GB	LOGG8	LOG68	LOG68
5	$*T(	$*T(	$*2(	S*2(	$*T)
6	986538	968538	986588	968538	998538
7	B27JP	B2J7P	B277P	B27PP	B277P
8	PC4#!	PC7#!	PC47!	PC4#1	PC4#!
9	GA!9%	GA!98	GA198	GA!98	GA19%
10	D*8XD	D*X*D	DX8XD	DX8XD	D*86D
11	969G)	669G)	696G)	669G)	669G)
12	EO((((	EO(()	EO((())	EO(())	EO()))
13	HEX09	HEX07	#EX09	H4X0P	HEX09
14	47S$	44S$$	47S$$	44SS$	44S$$
15	NVBR	NVR8	NVRB	NVRB	NVBB
16	69LBJ	69BLJ	99LBJ	69LBJ	69LJB
17	TXENE	TTENE	TXENN	TEXNE	TXENE

18	08%%Q	088%Q	0%8%Q	Q8%%Q	088%Q
19	LOP23	LOB23	LOP32	LOB32	LOB23
20	A79QA	A7Q9A	A790A	A970A	A970A

Test 28 Answer Sheet

	A	B	C	D	E
1	Ⓐ	Ⓑ	Ⓒ	Ⓓ	Ⓔ
2	Ⓐ	Ⓑ	Ⓒ	Ⓓ	Ⓔ
3	Ⓐ	Ⓑ	Ⓒ	Ⓓ	Ⓔ
4	Ⓐ	Ⓑ	Ⓒ	Ⓓ	Ⓔ
5	Ⓐ	Ⓑ	Ⓒ	Ⓓ	Ⓔ
6	Ⓐ	Ⓑ	Ⓒ	Ⓓ	Ⓔ
7	Ⓐ	Ⓑ	Ⓒ	Ⓓ	Ⓔ
8	Ⓐ	Ⓑ	Ⓒ	Ⓓ	Ⓔ
9	Ⓐ	Ⓑ	Ⓒ	Ⓓ	Ⓔ
10	Ⓐ	Ⓑ	Ⓒ	Ⓓ	Ⓔ
11	Ⓐ	Ⓑ	Ⓒ	Ⓓ	Ⓔ
12	Ⓐ	Ⓑ	Ⓒ	Ⓓ	Ⓔ
13	Ⓐ	Ⓑ	Ⓒ	Ⓓ	Ⓔ
14	Ⓐ	Ⓑ	Ⓒ	Ⓓ	Ⓔ
15	Ⓐ	Ⓑ	Ⓒ	Ⓓ	Ⓔ
16	Ⓐ	Ⓑ	Ⓒ	Ⓓ	Ⓔ
17	Ⓐ	Ⓑ	Ⓒ	Ⓓ	Ⓔ
18	Ⓐ	Ⓑ	Ⓒ	Ⓓ	Ⓔ
19	Ⓐ	Ⓑ	Ⓒ	Ⓓ	Ⓔ
20	Ⓐ	Ⓑ	Ⓒ	Ⓓ	Ⓔ

Test 29 Clerical Checking

This test measures speed and accuracy in checking detailed information. This type of test is often used to select clerical and administrative staff of all types.

Instructions: You are required to check that the hand-written information about sports centre bookings has been typed accurately. You should note any errors according to the following rules:

Fill in circle:

A = errors in name
B = errors in time
C = errors in date
D = errors in facilities
E = no errors

Indicate your answers by filling in completely the appropriate circles in the answer section.

Time guideline: There are 15 questions – see how many you can do in 3 minutes.

	Name	Time	Date	Tennis	Badminton	Gymnasium	Solarium
1	BROOK	8am	13.8	✓			
2	DRUMMOND	7am	24.8			✓	✓
3	CRIAG	9am	26.9		✓		
4	JONES	7.30am	15.9	✓		✓	
5	PATEL	3.25pm	7.11			✓	
6	BROWN	6.15pm	19.9				✓
7	HILL	7.10pm	17.8		✓		
8	PHILIPS	2.30pm	6.11	✓			✓
9	ADAMS	9.40am	17.9			✓	
10	SINGH	4.50pm	13.9		✓		
11	CHAN	11.25pm	9.10	✓			
12	YOUNG	10.30am	29.10			✓	✓
13	WILLIAMS	12.15am	18.11			✓	
14	SAMUELS	11.25am	26.10		✓		
15	MAN	10.30am	30.10	✓			✓

	Name	Time	Date	Facilities			
1	Brook	8am	23.8	🎾			
2	Drummond	7pm	24.8			🏋	
3	Craig	9am	26.9		🏸		
4	Jones	7.30am	15.9	🎾		🏋	
5	Patel	3.25pm	7.10		🏸		
6	Brown	6.15pm	19.9	🎾			
7	Hall	7.10am	25.9			🏋	
8	Philips	2.30am	6.11	🎾			☀
9	Adams	9.40am	17.9			🏋	
10	Singh	4.50pm	13.9		🏸		☀
11	Chan	1.25pm	9.10	🎾			
12	Young	10.30am	29.10			🏋	☀
13	Williams	12.15pm	18.11			🏋	
14	Samuels	11.25am	26.10	🎾			
15	Mann	10.40am	30.11	🎾			☀

SYMBOLS

SYMBOLS
TENNIS 🎾
BADMINTON 🏸
GYMNASIUM 🏋
SOLARIUM ☀

Test 29 Answer Sheet

	A	B	C	D	E
1	Ⓐ	Ⓑ	Ⓒ	Ⓓ	Ⓔ
2	Ⓐ	Ⓑ	Ⓒ	Ⓓ	Ⓔ
3	Ⓐ	Ⓑ	Ⓒ	Ⓓ	Ⓔ
4	Ⓐ	Ⓑ	Ⓒ	Ⓓ	Ⓔ
5	Ⓐ	Ⓑ	Ⓒ	Ⓓ	Ⓔ
6	Ⓐ	Ⓑ	Ⓒ	Ⓓ	Ⓔ
7	Ⓐ	Ⓑ	Ⓒ	Ⓓ	Ⓔ
8	Ⓐ	Ⓑ	Ⓒ	Ⓓ	Ⓔ
9	Ⓐ	Ⓑ	Ⓒ	Ⓓ	Ⓔ
10	Ⓐ	Ⓑ	Ⓒ	Ⓓ	Ⓔ
11	Ⓐ	Ⓑ	Ⓒ	Ⓓ	Ⓔ
12	Ⓐ	Ⓑ	Ⓒ	Ⓓ	Ⓔ
13	Ⓐ	Ⓑ	Ⓒ	Ⓓ	Ⓔ
14	Ⓐ	Ⓑ	Ⓒ	Ⓓ	Ⓔ
15	Ⓐ	Ⓑ	Ⓒ	Ⓓ	Ⓔ

Test 30 Computer Checking

This test measures your ability to check input information with the corresponding output, ie, the accurate recording of new data onto a VDU screen or computer printout. The information may be reordered in some way, requiring both checking and scanning ability, as well as an element of simple reasoning.

This type of test is often used to select school leavers and work-experienced applicants, both at the clerical and supervisory level, in a variety of organisations including building societies, banks, retailers and many public sector organisations. Examples of jobs include accounts clerks, clerical supervisors, mail order clerks and all office staff using VDUs.

Instructions: You are required to identify quickly and accurately whether the information has been correctly transferred to a VDU screen or computer printout. The output may be re-ordered in some way.

If there is an error in line 1 of the original document, fill in completely box A. If there is an error in line 2 of the original document, fill in completely box B. If there is an error in line 3 of the original document, fill in completely box C. If there is an error in line 4 of the original document, fill in completely box D. If there are no errors, fill in completely box E.

Time guideline: There is no official time guideline for this test. However, try to work through the questions as quickly and as accurately as possible.

1

Customer	582		
Invoice	X398		
Quantity	2	Size	36
Item	PD877	Value	18.99

2

Customer	379		
Invoice	X757		
Quantity	2	Size	10
Item	DX786	Value	9.50

3

Customer	323		
Invoice	Z819		
Quantity	3	Size	18
Item	ZX334	Value	36.90

4

Customer	414		
Invoice	B564		
Quantity	4	Size	18
Item	BT311	Value	31.99

114825 – 3			GENERAL COMMUNICATION AD5461		
RUN 4112			DATE 17 AUGUST		
INVOICE	CUSTOMER	QUANTITY	ITEM	SIZE	VALUE
X398	582	1	PD877	36	18.99
X757	397	2	DX786	12	9.50
Y213	664	1	LT468	40	25.00
Z819	323	3	ZX334	18	36.90
A742	443	5	BX021	2	12.50
B546	414	4	BT311	4	11.99
C611	452	1	BR121	6	2.49
C774	538	2	DX222	10	14.50
D775	543	1	BT223	11	15.00
D413	622	3	PT314	8	17.99
D276	422	6	ZD224	3	42.60
E119	123	3	LZ123	40	74.99
E772	232	1	DX223	10	14.22
E231	197	1	DX223	14	14.22
F332	772	1	BX223	4	15.00
F644	185	2	TD124	8	14.00
			END RUN 5421358 – 4		

Test 30 Answer Sheet

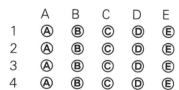

	A	B	C	D	E
1	Ⓐ	Ⓑ	Ⓒ	Ⓓ	Ⓔ
2	Ⓐ	Ⓑ	Ⓒ	Ⓓ	Ⓔ
3	Ⓐ	Ⓑ	Ⓒ	Ⓓ	Ⓔ
4	Ⓐ	Ⓑ	Ⓒ	Ⓓ	Ⓔ

Test 31 Coded Instructions

This test measures your ability to understand and follow written instructions when used in the form of coded language.

This type of test is often used to select school leavers and work-experienced applicants, both at the clerical and supervisory level in a variety of organisations including building societies, banks, retailers and many public sector organisations. Examples of jobs include accounts clerks, clerical supervisors, mail order clerks and all office staff using VDUs.

Instructions: The test consists of a series of passages containing instructions, each of which is followed by a number of questions. You are required to use the instructions in each passage to answer the questions which follow that passage. Indicate your answers each time by filling in completely the appropriate box A, B, C, D or E.

Time guideline: There is no official time guideline for this test. However, try to work through the questions as quickly and as accurately as possible.

Records Check

You are carrying out a computer check of personnel records.

If the staff member has left the organisation enter code L alone into the computer. For all staff members still present enter code P together with the appropriate check code below.

If the home address has changed enter code A: otherwise enter code B. If the home telephone number has changed enter code T. If the home telephone number is the same enter code C.

If the name of the staff member's doctor has changed enter code D: otherwise enter code N. If the doctor's telephone number has changed enter code R: if the telephone number is the same enter code S.

Code letters are to be entered in the sequence given above.

Which codes should be used to show the following records?

1   Employee number 1 is still a staff member. His address has changed but he has kept the same telephone number. There is no change to his doctor's details.

A   P A N S

B   A C N S

C   P A C N S

D   P A N C S

E   P A C S N

2 Employee number 2 changed her doctor a year ago but in the past month has left the organisation.

A   L R

B   L N R

C   R L

D   L

E   L R N

3 Employee number 3 is still a staff member. His address and telephone number are the same and so is the name of his doctor. However, his doctor is operating from a different address and telephone number.

A   P B C R

B   P B C R N

C   P C N

D   L P B C R

E   P B C N R

4 Employee number 4 is still a staff member. Her address and telephone number are unchanged. Her doctor's name and telephone number are unchanged.

A   P B N

B   P B C N S

C   P N S B C

D   P A C N S

E   P B T N S

Test 31 Answer Sheet

	A	B	C	D	E
1	Ⓐ	Ⓑ	Ⓒ	Ⓓ	Ⓔ
2	Ⓐ	Ⓑ	Ⓒ	Ⓓ	Ⓔ
3	Ⓐ	Ⓑ	Ⓒ	Ⓓ	Ⓔ
4	Ⓐ	Ⓑ	Ⓒ	Ⓓ	Ⓔ

Test 32 Following Instructions

This test measures your ability to understand and follow written instructions. The topic covered is relevant to a technical environment although no prior knowledge of technical words is assumed.

This type of test is often used to select staff for modern apprenticeship schemes and other technically orientated jobs. It is also used to select graduates applying to work in applied technical areas, for example, electronics technicians, electrical technicians and research technicians.

Instructions: In this test you are given a written passage containing instructions. Use the instructions in the passage to answer the questions which follow. Indicate your answers each time by filling in completely the appropriate circle A, B, C or D.

Time guideline: There is no official time guideline for this test. However, try to work through the questions as quickly and as accurately as possible.

Photocopier Operation

Push the SORTER switch if the sorter is to be used to collate the copies (i.e. separate them into sets). The sort indicator is lit when this switch is on. If the lamp flashes, check the position of the sorter.

NO SORT mode   up to 99 copies can be made, all delivered to the top bin.

SORT mode   15 copies can be made from each original. The original can be up to 30 pages long. One copy of each original is delivered to each bin.

Originals should be arranged in reverse order when using the SORT mode.

---

1   What should you do if the sorter indicator flashes?

    A Push the SORTER switch.
    B Check the position of the sorter.
    C Disconnect the sorter.
    D Collate manually.

2   What is the maximum number of pages a document can have if the sorter is to be used?

    A 15.
    B 99.
    C 30.
    D No limit.

Test 32 Answer Sheet

	A	B	C	D
1	Ⓐ	Ⓑ	Ⓒ	Ⓓ
2	Ⓐ	Ⓑ	Ⓒ	Ⓓ

Answers to accuracy tests

Test 27 Basic Checking

	A	B	C	D	E
1		Ⓑ	Ⓒ	●	Ⓔ
2	Ⓐ	Ⓑ	●	Ⓓ	●
3	Ⓐ	●	Ⓒ	●	Ⓔ
4		Ⓑ	●	Ⓓ	Ⓔ
5	Ⓐ	●	●	Ⓓ	Ⓔ
6	Ⓐ	Ⓑ	●	Ⓓ	●
7	Ⓐ	●	Ⓒ	Ⓓ	●
8	Ⓐ	Ⓑ	Ⓒ	●	●
9	Ⓐ	●	Ⓒ	●	Ⓔ
10		Ⓑ	●	Ⓓ	Ⓔ
11		Ⓑ	Ⓒ	Ⓓ	●
12	Ⓐ	Ⓑ	●	Ⓓ	●
13		Ⓑ	Ⓒ	●	Ⓔ
14	Ⓐ	Ⓑ	●	●	Ⓔ

Test 28 Computer Checking

	A	B	C	D	E
1		Ⓑ	Ⓒ	●	Ⓔ
2	Ⓐ	●	Ⓒ	Ⓓ	●
3		Ⓑ	●	Ⓓ	Ⓔ
4	Ⓐ	Ⓑ	Ⓒ	●	●
5		●	Ⓒ	Ⓓ	Ⓔ
6	Ⓐ	●	Ⓒ	●	Ⓔ
7	Ⓐ	Ⓑ	●	Ⓓ	●
8		Ⓑ	Ⓒ	Ⓓ	●
9	Ⓐ	●	Ⓒ	●	Ⓔ
10	Ⓐ	Ⓑ	●	●	Ⓔ
11	Ⓐ	●	Ⓒ	●	Ⓔ
12	Ⓐ	Ⓑ	●	●	Ⓔ
13		Ⓑ	Ⓒ	Ⓓ	●
14	Ⓐ	●	Ⓒ	Ⓓ	●
15	Ⓐ	Ⓑ	●	●	Ⓔ
16		Ⓑ	Ⓒ	●	Ⓔ
17		Ⓑ	Ⓒ	Ⓓ	●
18	Ⓐ	●	Ⓒ	Ⓓ	●
19	Ⓐ	●	Ⓒ	Ⓓ	●
20	Ⓐ	Ⓑ	Ⓒ	●	●

Test 29 Clerical Checking

	A	B	C	D	E
1	Ⓐ	Ⓑ	●	Ⓓ	Ⓔ
2	Ⓐ	●	Ⓒ	●	Ⓔ
3	●	Ⓑ	Ⓒ	Ⓓ	Ⓔ
4	Ⓐ	Ⓑ	Ⓒ	Ⓓ	●
5	Ⓐ	Ⓑ	●	●	Ⓔ
6	Ⓐ	Ⓑ	Ⓒ	●	Ⓔ
7	●	●	●	●	Ⓔ
8	Ⓐ	●	Ⓒ	Ⓓ	Ⓔ
9	Ⓐ	Ⓑ	Ⓒ	Ⓓ	●
10	Ⓐ	Ⓑ	Ⓒ	●	Ⓔ
11	Ⓐ	●	Ⓒ	Ⓓ	Ⓔ
12	Ⓐ	Ⓑ	Ⓒ	Ⓓ	●
13	Ⓐ	●	Ⓒ	Ⓓ	Ⓔ
14	Ⓐ	Ⓑ	Ⓒ	●	Ⓔ
15	●	●	●	Ⓓ	Ⓔ

Test 30 Computer Checking

	A	B	C	D	E
1	Ⓐ	Ⓑ	●	Ⓓ	Ⓔ
2	●	Ⓑ	●	Ⓓ	Ⓔ
3	Ⓐ	Ⓑ	Ⓒ	Ⓓ	●
4	Ⓐ	●	●	●	Ⓔ

Test 31 Coded Instructions

	A	B	C	D	E
1	Ⓐ	Ⓑ	●	Ⓓ	Ⓔ
2	Ⓐ	Ⓑ	Ⓒ	●	Ⓔ
3	Ⓐ	Ⓑ	Ⓒ	Ⓓ	●
4	Ⓐ	●	Ⓒ	Ⓓ	Ⓔ

Test 32 Following Instructions

	A	B	C	D
1	Ⓐ	●	Ⓒ	Ⓓ
2	Ⓐ	Ⓑ	●	Ⓓ

How to improve your performance

- Use catalogues and timetables.
- Check the football or financial results.
- Play games involving checking numbers and letters.
- Read lots of instructions for using things, for example, a digital clock or video recorder.
- Read lots of instructions for making or repairing things, for example, making a cake or fixing a fuse, and check that you understand what you're reading.
- Try looking at manuals and instructions for games, appliances and computers.
- Accuracy tests demand a very high level of concentration, so treat yourself to a short break every now and then. Sit up straight, shut your eyes and take a few deep breaths, just for 20 seconds or so. This will help you stay alert, relax you a little, and give your eyes and brain a well deserved rest.

CHAPTER ELEVEN

Combination Tests

So far, all the psychometric tests in this book have been very specific; each one of them measuring a certain ability, be it verbal, numerical, mechanical and so on.

However, out there in the big wide world, there are employers who do not use accredited and well researched psychometric tests from well established test publishers like SHL – they make up their own tests themselves. I have decided to include one of these tests.

It's what I call a *combination* test because it is a mixture of verbal reasoning, number problems and abstract puzzles, with one or two spatial reasoning questions thrown in for good measure. The company that uses it recruits software engineers.

Now, you might be thinking, 'How can a test like this sort out potentially good software engineers from bad ones? What relevance has knowing in which month of the year the 47th week appears to the skills needed by the IT industry?'

The answer is surprising – there isn't really any relevance at all! The company who uses this test isn't trying to measure verbal ability, nor numerical ability, nor general knowledge. What they are interested in is **speed of thought**. They want people who can think quickly.

In actual fact, speed of thought is an essential attribute for a software engineer. In a commercial world, projects completed quickly mean larger profits and an enhanced reputation for the company in question.

And there's another reason I've included this test – it's quite good fun!

Test 33 Combination Test

Instructions: The objective of the test is to answer as many questions as possible correctly in 14 minutes. Simply tick the letter corresponding to your answer underneath each question.

Although many of the questions are not particularly difficult, you'll need all the concentration you can muster to beat the clock, so sit somewhere quiet where you won't be disturbed.

Time guide: There are 44 questions. See how many you can do in 14 minutes. The answers are at the end of the chapter.

1   The 47th week of the year is in:

    (a)   December
    (b)   November
    (c)   September
    (d)   June
    (e)   January

2   Does IQ stand for Intellectual Quotient?

    (a)   Yes
    (b)   No

3   Which word is different from the rest?

    (a)   whimsical
    (b)   playful
    (c)   capricious
    (d)   uncanny
    (e)   comical

4   Pick the number that follows the pattern set by the series:

    0 1 3 6 10 __

    (a)   6
    (b)   14
    (c)   15
    (d)   16

5   Which one of these forms does not belong with the rest?

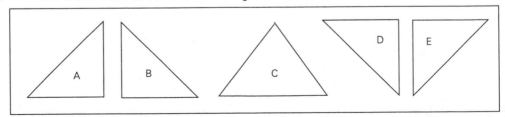

6   STRANGE is the opposite of:

(a)   similar
(b)   familiar
(c)   peculiar
(d)   obstinate
(e)   happy

7   One orange cost 12 pence. A dozen and a half oranges will cost:

(a)   £1.44
(b)   £2.16
(c)   £0.30
(d)   £1.80
(e)   £2.06

8   HARSH is the opposite of:

(a)   stern
(b)   mild
(c)   severe
(d)   warm
(e)   weather

9   OBVIOUS is the opposite of:

(a)   apparent
(b)   clear
(c)   obscure
(d)   visible
(e)   conspicuous

10   Which of the following numbers does not fit in with the pattern of this series?

64   54   42   31   20

(a)   64
(b)   54
(c)   42
(d)   31
(e)   20

11   Which one of these forms does not belong with the rest?

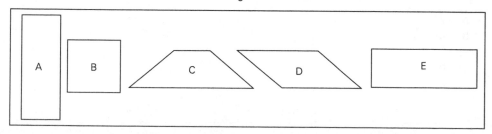

12   If most Gannucks are Dorks and most Gannucks are Xorgs, the statement that some Dorks are Xorgs is:

(a)   True
(b)   False
(c)   Indeterminable from data

13   A car dealer spent £20,000 for some used cars. He sold them for £27,500 making an average of £1,500 on each car. How many cars did he sell?

(a)   4
(b)   11
(e)   5
(d)   15
(e)   7

14   What is the opposite of ABDICATE?

(a)   occupy
(b)   edit
(c)   court
(d)   attempt
(e)   abandon

15   If you put the following words into a meaningful statement, what would the last word be?

(a)   fall
(b)   a
(c)   before
(d)   pride
(e)   comes

16   Which of the following words is related to SOUND as FOOD is to MOUTH?

(a)   ear
(b)   stomach
(c)   music
(d)   orchestra
(e)   throat

17   Tom and Harry caught a dozen fish. Harry caught twice as many as Tom. How many did Tom catch?

(a)   2
(b)   4
(c)   8
(d)   6
(e)   3

18 Which of the following numbers doesn't fit the sequence?

13 18 14 19 15 21 16

(a) 13
(b) 18
(c) 14
(d) 19
(e) 15
(f) 21
(g) 16

19 Which letter does not belong in the sequence?

C F J M Q U

(a) C
(b) F
(c) J
(d) M
(e) Q
(f) U

20 If George met Gertrude and Gertrude met Ralph, then the statement that George and Ralph did not meet is:

(a) True
(b) False
(c) Indeterminable

21 If it takes four bricklayers an hour to build a wall, how long will it take five of them to build the same wall?

(a) 90 minutes
(b) 45 minutes
(c) 50 minutes
(d) 48 minutes
(e) 40 minutes

22 What is the opposite of REPUDIATE?

(a) encourage
(b) crime
(c) endorse
(d) disappoint
(e) halt

23 The first four forms are alike in a certain way. Pick the numbered form that is also alike:

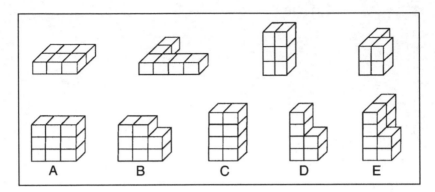

24 If Bob is older than Harry and Harry is older than Sue, the statement that Sue is younger than Bob is:

(a) True
(b) False
(c) Indeterminable from data

25 What is the opposite of IMBUE?

(a) prize
(b) tasteful
(c) texture
(d) invest
(e) clear

26 A bag of coffee beans costs £30 and contains 100 possible servings. However, typical wastage averages 25%. For how much must the proprietor sell a cup of coffee to make a 150% profit per bag?

(a) £1.25
(b) £0.75
(c) £1.00
(d) £2.00
(e) none of these answers are right

27 If a pair of trousers takes one-and-a-half as much cloth as a shirt, and the total cloth used for the trousers and the shirt is £50, how much does the cloth for the trousers cost?

(a) £25
(b) £20
(c) £30
(d) £40
(e) none of these answers

28 Complete the comparison: BOOK is to LIBRARY as PAINTING is to

    (a)   artists
    (b)   curator
    (c)   easel
    (d)   gallery
    (e)   building

29 What meaning do the following two statements have?

Don't put all your eggs in one basket.
Don't count your chickens before they hatch.

    (a)   same
    (b)   opposite
    (c)   neither the same nor opposite

30 Which one of the following numbers doesn't fit the pattern?

5/8   9/24   1/4   2/16   0

    (a)   5/8
    (b)   9/24
    (c)   1/4
    (d)   2/16
    (e)   0

31 Complete the comparison: BISHOP is to CHESS as SOLDIER is to

    (a)   battlefield
    (b)   war
    (c)   government
    (d)   army
    (e)   gun

32 Pick the piece that's missing from the puzzle.

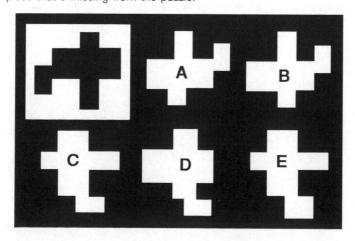

33   The following statements:

Hindsight is always 20/20
Can't see the trees for the forest

(a)   are the same in meaning
(b)   are opposite in meaning
(c)   are neither the same nor opposite in meaning

34   A zoo has some lions and some ostriches. The zoo keeper counted 15 heads and 50 legs. How
many lions were there?

(a)   9
(b)   10
(c)   11
(d)   12
(e)   13
(f)   14

35   A sushi restaurant buys twenty fish for £10 each. The owner knows that 50% of the fish will go
bad before being served. Each fish creates 10 servings. What price must they charge per serving
in order to make a 100% profit on their initial investment?

(a)   £4
(b)   £2
(c)   £3
(d)   £6
(e)   £20

36   The words SURREPTITIOUS and SUSPICIOUS mean:

(a)   same
(b)   opposite
(c)   neither the same nor opposite

37   Three partners venture on a project. They pro-rate their (potential) profits over their £11,000
investment. Dan invests twice as much as Pete. Pete invests 50% more than Phil. If the venture
breaks even how much does Phil get back?

(a)   £6000
(b)   £2500
(c)   £2000
(d)   £3666.66
(e)   0

38 A basketball player shoots 33% from the foul line. How many shots must he take to make 100 baskets?

(a) 300
(b) 301
(c) 304
(d) 100
(e) 333

39 All Nerds are Jerks and some Nerds are Geeks. A few Geeks are BrainMasters, therefore all Brainmasters are Jerks.

(a) True
(b) False
(c) Indeterminable from data

40 A submarine averages 10 miles an hour under water and 25 miles per hour on the surface. How many hours will it take it to make a 350 mile trip if it goes two-and-a-half times faster on the surface?

(a) 10
(b) 15
(c) 35
(d) 20
(e) 65

41 A man was given eight pound coins. However, one of them was fake and he did not know if the fake coin weighed more or less than the other coins. What is the minimum number of weighings that it would take to guarantee him finding the counterfeit coin? Assume a balance scale is used.

(a) 2
(b) 3
(c) 7
(d) 12
(e) Indeterminable from data

42 Which number does not fit within the following sequence?

1/5 1/6 1/8 1/10 1/15 1/30

(a) 1/5
(b) 1/6
(c) 1/8
(d) 1/10
(e) 1/15
(f) 1/30

43   At the end of a banquet 10 people shake hands with each other. How many handshakes will there be in total?

(a)   100
(b)   90
(c)   45
(d)   20
(e)   50

44   Complete the comparison: SOLICITOR is to ADVISER as SYCOPHANT is to:

(a)   ruffian
(b)   fawner
(c)   nobleman
(d)   blackmailer
(e)   flautist

Answers to combination test

Now here are the answers. For your information, the company who uses this test considers a score of 30 or more *correct* answers good enough to move a candidate on to the next stage in the recruitment process. No one has ever scored full marks.

1 b	23 d
2 b	24 a
3 d	25 e
4 c	26 c
5 c	27 c
6 b	28 d
7 b	29 c
8 b	30 a
9 c	31 b
10 b	32 c
11 c	33 c
12 a	34 b
13 c	35 a
14 a	36 c
15 a	37 c
16 a	38 c
17 b	39 c
18 f	40 d
19 f	41 b
20 c	42 c
21 d	43 c
22 c	44 b

CHAPTER TWELVE

Personality Questionnaires

What are personality questionnaires?

Personality questionnaires are psychometric tests which assess the different aspects of personality and character which are relevant to the world of work, for example:

- ✓ motivation
- ✓ thinking style
- ✓ problem solving
- ✓ preferred working style
- ✓ feelings and emotions
- ✓ business awareness
- ✓ interpersonal skills
- ✓ leadership ability
- ✓ managerial, professional or entrepreneurial qualities
- ✓ communication skills.

However, personality questionnaires, or 'inventories' as they are sometimes called, are not tests in the true sense of the word, for two reasons:

1. there are no right or wrong answers
2. they are not timed.

What they are, though, is popular. Written by occupational psychologists and administered by trained HR personnel, their use has increased dramatically in the last few years. From shelf-stacker to director, apply for a job with any medium to large organisation (commercial or otherwise) and you will probably be asked to complete a personality questionnaire.

The results of the personality questionnaire could determine your overall suitability to work for a particular organisation, or place you in an appropriate department or team once the decision has already been made to employ you. They're also very useful for recruiters, because it gives them something to talk about when they interview you.

When will I be required to complete a personality questionnaire?

At any time during the recruitment process. Some companies put them on their application forms and/or web sites, thereby using the personality questionnaire to eliminate candidates they consider to be unsuitable right at the start.

Others leave the personality questionnaire until later in the process, perhaps when you go along to be interviewed, or when you attend an assessment centre. (For an explanation of this see Chapter 1 – What Are Psychometric Tests?)

Will I be asked any very personal questions?

No. They are not puzzles or quizzes of the magazine variety; they never ask you about your favourite foods or your love life. Personality questionnaires used in recruitment simply assess aspects of your personality and character as they relate to the working environment, or a specific job.

What sort of questions will I be asked?

To give you a flavour of what to expect I have included two different practice personality questionnaires for you to try. As with all the other tests in this book (with the exception of the Combination Test) they are genuine practice tests from the biggest test publisher in the world, SHL Group plc.

The only difference between these tests and the real thing is that real personality questionnaires have more questions.

Test 34 Rating Statements

In this test you are asked to rate yourself on a number of different phrases or statements. After reading each statement mark your answer according to the following rules:

Fill in circle 1   If you strongly disagree with the statement
Fill in circle 2   If you disagree with the statement
Fill in circle 3   If you are unsure
Fill in circle 4   If you agree with the statement
Fill in circle 5   If you strongly agree with the statement

The first statement has already been completed for you. The person has agreed that 'I enjoy meeting new people' is an accurate description of him/herself.

Now try questions 2 to 6 for yourself by completely filling in the circle that is most true for you.

		Strongly disagree	Disagree	Unsure	Agree	Strongly agree
1	I enjoy meeting new people	①	②	③	●	⑤
2	I like helping people	①	②	③	④	⑤
3	I sometimes make mistakes	①	②	③	④	⑤
4	I don't mind taking risks	①	②	③	④	⑤
5	I'm easily disappointed	①	②	③	④	⑤
6	I enjoy repairing things	①	②	③	④	⑤

Test 35 Making Choices

This personality questionnaire has a different format. You are given a block of 4 statements: A, B, C and D. You must choose the statement which you think is most true or typical of you in your everyday behaviour, and you must **also** choose the statement which is least true or typical of you.

Indicate your choices by filling in the appropriate circle in the row marked 'M' (for most) and in the next row 'L' (for least).

The first question has been completed as an example of what to do. The person has chosen, 'Enjoys organising people' as most true or typical, and 'Seeks variety' as being least true or typical. Now try questions 2, 3 and 4 yourself.

I am the sort of person who...

1   A   Has a wide circle of friends

   B   Enjoys organising people   M   Ⓐ   ●   Ⓒ   Ⓓ

   C   Relaxes easily   L   Ⓐ   Ⓑ   Ⓒ   ●

   D   Seeks variety

2   A   Helps people with their problems

   B   Develops new approaches   M   Ⓐ   Ⓑ   Ⓒ   Ⓓ

   C   Has lots of energy   L   Ⓐ   Ⓑ   Ⓒ   Ⓓ

   D   Enjoys social activities

3   A   Has lots of new ideas

   B   Feels calm   M   Ⓐ   Ⓑ   Ⓒ   Ⓓ

   C   Likes to understand things   L   Ⓐ   Ⓑ   Ⓒ   Ⓓ

   D   Is easy to get on with

4   A   Enjoys organising events

   B   Sometimes gets angry   M   Ⓐ   Ⓑ   Ⓒ   Ⓓ

   C   Is talkative   L   Ⓐ   Ⓑ   Ⓒ   Ⓓ

   D   Resolves conflicts at work

I'm finding it hard to decide which statement is least like me – what should I do?

I agree, it is difficult. In the past, when you took a personality test, there would always be several answer choices which stood out a mile as being the wrong ones. But not any more.

Here are some other examples of statements taken from 21st century personality questionnaires:

- Changes tasks willingly and grasps new ideas quickly.
- Communicates equally well with customers and colleagues.
- Pursues tasks energetically.
- Shares all relevant and useful information with the team.

You can see the problem. Which of these statements should you choose as being the *least* like you? They all describe qualities you'd imagine any employer would find highly desirable.

This test, and others like it are extremely clever because they are impossible to fudge. There are no obvious right or wrong answers. And the fact that there are no blindingly obvious 'least like you' answers, forces you to think hard about yourself and be honest.

And that's exactly what organisations who use these tests want – honesty.

Is it possible to cheat?

Modern personality questionnaires have sophisticated built-in mechanisms which can spot any deliberate lying or inconsistency only too easily. If you try to second guess the examiners by picking the answers you think they're looking for, your questionnaire is likely to be regarded as invalid, and your application rejected. Your only choice is to answer the questions as truthfully and honestly as you can.

Even if you manage to bluff or lie your way through the personality questionnaire, you'll still be found out. Interviewers like to talk about the results of the test, and then they often ask whether you agree with the results or not.

For example, if you've tried to give the impression that you have, say, leadership ability, what are you going to say when your interviewer asks you to describe your leadership experience?

Besides, personality questionnaires are also about fitting the right people into the right jobs. By answering honestly, you're more likely to land a job that you enjoy and can do well.

How to improve your performance

With every other type of psychometric test I have been able to give you some suggestions as to how to improve your performance. However, with personality questionnaires, there are no tricks of the trade or useful exercises you can do. As I have already said, the most important thing to do is to **be yourself.** Remember:

- Personality questionnaires do not have right or wrong answers. You don't have to worry about passing or failing – just concentrate on being honest, truthful and accurate.
- Make sure you answer all the questions. There may seem like a lot of them, but it is necessary to complete the whole test.
- Personality questionnaires do not have time limits, but try to work your way through reasonably quickly. This is particularly useful when being asked to decide which 'qualities' are most or least like you. Here, your intuitive answer is usually the most accurate – if you sit and think too hard you'll find the questions much more difficult.
- Some questions may seem completely irrelevant – don't worry about this. Just answer as truthfully as you can and move on.
- Many questions ask you about the way you typically behave in a work situation. If you have no formal work experience, think about how you behave in similar situations such as voluntary work, school or college.

After taking a personality questionnaire, you should be offered the chance to discuss the results. Use the opportunity to find out as much about yourself as you can. Even if you are not offered that particular job, a better understanding of your strengths and limitations is always useful.

CHAPTER THIRTEEN

What Else Do Psychometric Tests Test?

As we've seen in Part 2, there are many different types of psychometric test. Some measure your ability to work or reason in a certain way, some claim to analyse aspects of your personality and character.

But there are three things that **all** psychometric tests measure.

◆ First, your ability to turn up on time, settle down, concentrate and work hard for a reasonable amount of time.

◆ Second, your ability (or lack of it) to follow instructions and work neatly – absolutely essential if you want to score any points at all on any kind of psychometric test.

◆ And lastly, of course, your ability to understand precisely what you are being asked to do.

These are qualities **every** organisation looks for in its staff. They want your timekeeping to be reliable. They want you to be able to settle down and work quickly and effectively and not mess about. They want you to respect the organisation's culture and follow laid-down procedures, not make up your own rules as you go along. They want you to get on with your job and not waste time pretending to be ill, gossiping or playing computer games. Asking a bit much, I suppose, but some people are unable (or unwilling) to do any of these things.

Your references may not be entirely honest. Your CV may exaggerate your achievements. You may be able to impress whole armies of interviewers with a show of confidence, charm, friendliness and even sex-appeal. But with a psychometric test, you are on your own. You can see why employers like them so much.

PART THREE
Psychometric Tests in Context

CHAPTER FOURTEEN

Keeping It All In Perspective

However much psychometric tests are lauded as the fail-safe, scientific method of selecting the best candidates, and however widespread the use of them grows, I really don't think employers will ever come to rely on them completely. The good news is that psychometric tests will always be just a part of the recruitment process, a powerful tool but not the only one.

You'll never be hired purely on the strength of a test – once you've got through the initial stages of a selection process (which shouldn't be a problem now you have this book) you will always have your chance to impress at an interview.

And for those of you who are still quaking at the knees, let me reiterate:

1. In a psychometric test you do not have to score 100% to pass. Many organisations set the 'pass' level as low as 50%. The whole point of the test is to eliminate candidates who are totally hopeless, so they can concentrate on the rest of you.

2. Most ability-type tests are not designed to be finished in the time set. Giving you more questions than you can reasonably cope with in the allotted time is a deliberate ploy. Taking a psychometric test is meant to be stressful.

3. You can improve your test performance considerably by familiarisation and practice – the reason you bought this book!

CHAPTER FIFTEEN

Avoiding Psychometric Tests Altogether

What if, despite hours of practice and bank accounts full of therapy, the thought of taking a psychometric test still makes you feel like hiding under the bed? Is it possible to avoid taking psychometric tests altogether?

Well, given that a growing number of companies subject potential employees to some sort of testing in addition to the traditional face-to-face interview, it may not be possible to do this – especially if you are applying to large companies.

However, there are a number of possibilities that do spring to mind. The most obvious one is to apply for a job with an SME.

Working for an SME

Before you decide that the only organisations worth working for are BIG ones, consider the alternative. A smaller company (an SME) may have just as much, or even more to offer.

Note: The definition of an SME varies according to who you ask! To give you a rough guide, an SME is usually an organisation which employs up to 50 people, and/or a turnover up to £20 million. So 'small' can mean anything from absolutely tiny, to really quite large, well-established and vastly successful companies.

Here are just some of the advantages of working for an SME:

✓ More responsibility, earlier on.
✓ The chance to work directly with the directors/owners of the business.
✓ Greater variety of work.
✓ The opportunity to learn every aspect of how a business works.
✓ Reasonable starting salaries (SMEs know they have to compete with the big boys).

✓ A real chance to be a big fish in a small pond.

It's also much easier to land a job with an SME than a large company because their recruitment processes are usually simpler. After you've submitted your CV and letter, huge numbers of SMEs still rely on a couple of interviews to pick their people. Of course, I'm not absolutely guaranteeing that. An ability test to determine your suitability for a specific job (for example, having to analyse a set of figures when applying for a statistics job) is still a very real possibility. But with an SME you are certainly less likely to be given a psychometric test, and very unlikely to be required to attend an assessment centre, give a presentation, or have your Lego building capabilities scrutinised.

Just why this should be so isn't clear. Perhaps it's because most SMEs (and certainly the smaller ones) do not possess full-time personnel departments. Perhaps it's because they simply don't have the time and resources to drag the recruitment process out for longer than absolutely necessary. Perhaps it's because directors of small firms, who often interview applicants themselves, are confident about their abilities to pick the right people without recourse to additional methods of selection.

If I were looking for a job, and a good one at that, I'd definitely go for an SME.

Working for yourself

Becoming self-employed could be an area you haven't even considered. It would certainly appeal if you are the sort of person who:

◆ likes the autonomy of making his or her own decisions
◆ is happy to work alone
◆ is extremely determined
◆ is prepared to forgo the security of a guaranteed salary.

Successful entrepreneurs also have to be very organised and hard working. They are frequently charismatic and creative risk-takers with leadership ability. They are usually confident, always intelligent, and they need to be able to get on well with others.

And because fashions, industries and economies are constantly changing, successful entrepreneurs have to be prepared to face a never-ending stream of challenges and problems. However, if you have a product or service that people want, and you are able to offer a professional and reliable service, there's every chance that, in time, you could become very successful indeed.

Of course, working for yourself has its downsides too. You will have to market your product or service in order to find customers – which can be very difficult. You may not have a boss telling you what to do, but you'll still have masters: fickle customers, unreliable suppliers, and whoever you've borrowed money from looking over your shoulder. Furthermore, it may take a long time to build up a regular clientele, which means your income stays lower for longer than your employed friends.

But one thing is certain: if you work for yourself, no one will ever expect you to take a psychometric test!

For help and advice on becoming self-employed, try:

- *www.bt.com/sme or www.bt.com/getstarted*
- Small Business Service.
- The DTI.
- Federation of Small Businesses.
- Your relevant trade organisation.
- Plus: talk to people you know who are already running their own businesses. Ask them about their experiences and the problems they've faced. They'll soon bring you down to earth if your expectations are unrealistic.

Resources

Help and information on the Internet

www.shldirect.com
Attractive site offers careers guidance, help with the assessment process and free practice ability tests and personality questionnaires.

www.majon.com/iq.html
Another interesting US site includes IQ test selection area, with information on the main US postgraduate college entrance exams (all high-level psychometric tests) including GRE, LSAT, GMAT, MCAT and SAT.

www.psychometrics.co.uk
Interesting information about psychometric tests, assessment centres, cv writing, etc.

www.testingroom.com
US site offering free tests on topics such as personality, career values, career interest inventories and career competencies.

www.9types.com
Entertaining personality questionnaire site.

www.advisorteam.com
Take the free Keirsey Temperament Sorter and discover whethere you are an Artisan, Guardian, Rational or Idealist. Also IQ tests and free newsletter.

www.allthetests.com
Losts of fun IQ, memory and personality tests, plus help with SAT, GMAT, GRE, LSAT and MCAT tests.

www.2h.com/iq-tests.html
Fun IQ, entrepreneur and personality tests.

www.prospects.ac.uk
Extensive site for graduates, with loads of career and job-hunting advice, plus jobs.

www.careersa-z.co.uk
Information on hundreds of different careers.

www.hobsons.co.uk
A top site for career advice, information on employers, graduate vacancies, placement work and term-time jobs.

http://work.guardian.co.uk
Great interactive job site has free practice psychometric tests plus lots of work-related news.

www.hotrecruit.co.uk
Thousands of part-time and temporary jobs, including lots of extraordinary and simply crazy jobs. You can check out the jobs without having to register, which makes a change.

www.jobserve.com
Good recruitment site for a multitude of different industries, especially IT.

University web sites often have lots of useful career information and job hunting help, especially for graduates. Many include tips on taking psychometric tests. Some good ones are:

www.keele.ac.uk
http://www.graduatecareersonline.com (Manchester University)
www.careers.lon.ac.uk (London University)
http://www.shef.ac.uk/careers.students/applying (Sheffield University)

More links to useful sites, good recruitment and career information can be found on my website www.shavick.com on the career link page – or go directly to *http:// www.shavick.com/careerlinkpage.htm*

Further Reading

Psychometric Tests for Graduates, Andrea Shavick (How To Books, 2003)

Landing Your First Job, Andrea Shavick (Kogan Page). Step-by-step guide through the job-hunting maze from CV to interview technique. View the virtual CV at *www.shavick.com*

Surfing Your Career, Hilary Nickell (How To Books, 2nd end., 2002)

The Internet Job Search Handbook, Andrea Semple and Matt Haig (How To Books, 2001)

Write a Winning CV, Julie-Ann Amos (How To Books, 2nd edn., 2003)

Writing a CV That Works, Paul McGee (How To Books 2nd edn., 2002)

High Powered CVs, Rachel Bishop-Firth (How To Books, 2nd edn., 2002)

The Ultimate CV for Managers and Professionals, Rachel Bishop-Firth (How To Books, 2nd edn., 2004)

Successful Interviews Every Time, Dr Rob Yeung (How To Books, 2nd edn., 2004)

The Career Change Handbook, Graham Green (How To Books, 2003)

Turn Your Degree into a Career, Benjamin Scott and Dr Michael Collins (How To Books, 2003)

Succeeding at Interviews, Judith Verity (How To Books, 3rd edn., 2004)

Passing That Interview, Judith Johnstone (How To Books 5th edn., 2001)

Handling Tough Job Interviews, Julie-Ann Amos (How To Books, 2nd edn., 2004)

Be Prepared! Getting Ready for Interviews, Julie-Ann Amos (How To Books, 2nd edn., 2004)

The Redundancy Survivor's Field Guide, Graham Till (How To Books, 2nd edn., 2003)

Index